WORDS ALONE

THE TEACHING AND USAGE OF
ENGLISH IN CONTEMPORARY IRELAND

T0304424

Words Alone

The Teaching and Usage of English in Contemporary Ireland

EDITED BY

*Denis Bates, Conor Galvin
Desmond Swan & Kevin Williams*

University College Dublin Press
Preas Choláiste Ollscoile Bhaile Átha Cliath

First published 2000 by University College Dublin Press,
Newman House, 86 St Stephen's Green, Dublin 2, Ireland

Published with the assistance of the In-Career Development Unit
which is co-funded by the Department of Education and Science and the
European Social Fund.

ISBN 1 900621 33 9

Typeset in New Aster & Optima by Elaine Shiels, Bantry, Co. Cork, Ireland
Index by John Loftus
Printed in Ireland by Colour Books, Dublin

Contents

vi

Contents

Preface

The recent publication of *Draft Guidelines for Teachers of English* by the National Council for Curriculum and Assessment, and the ongoing reviews of the Primary School and Junior and Leaving Certificate curricula in English, together emphasise the need for teachers at all levels to keep themselves fully up to date in this subject. The papers in this volume will help them do so, whilst informing other readers on the very rapid pace of change in the language they use every hour of the day, on its range and complexity, and why teaching it is no simple matter.

Indeed English is the least subject-like of subjects and teaching it to Irish students is, in part, teaching them who they are. Language is communication and identity, it is living and learning, it is working and loving; learning one's vernacular is learning all of these, since the limits of my language are the limits of my world. Few areas of the curriculum are as significant as English therefore, whether seen in terms of individual development or the transmission of culture, or the economic welfare of society. By the same token, there must be few areas of education in which so many conflicts converge, as shown in many of these papers. Some of the conflicts are cultural in origin; if their language is arguably the most significant legacy of the English to Ireland, its literature in the same language in turn may well be Ireland's greatest gift to the English. Other sources of conflict centre on the methodologies of teaching virtually every aspect of English, while still others are ideological, for example progressive approaches versus the conservative 'back- to- basics' movement. Recent years testify to the highly political connotations these words now bear within education.

Kevin Williams's paper succinctly indicates the diversity of the task of the teacher of English, in light of some of these controversies, ranging across all the major areas, and showing that it is both an awesome and a humbling role. Brian Cox's cautionary tale from England and Wales and Declan Kiberd's Ireland-centred response together illustrate just how political is this area of curriculum, in all countries. Professor Kiberd traces the ambivalent twists and turns of independent Ireland's educational masters in the area of the English curriculum, while Professor Cox, as a participant observer at the birth of the British National Curriculum, outlines his experience of the difficulty of ensuring that educational principles are given precedence over the political.

Achieving even average mastery of the English language may be the most complex learning task of a lifetime – it includes gaining a vocabulary of perhaps 50,000 words, a thousand grammatical constructions and 300 ways of combining its 44 letter sounds into sequences (Crystal, 1997). First come the skills of listening and speaking, and, as one of Mary Howard's seven-year-old pupils pointed out 'There's no point in speaking, teacher, if nobody is listening'. In the age of Walkmans, video-conferencing, and a tv set in every room, the added importance of specific lessons in listening and speaking in every school is clear. This contribution and the emerging emphasis on oracy in the Leaving Certificate are therefore all the more timely. Elizabeth O'Gorman's paper deals expertly with the teaching of a central language skill – reading comprehension – especially to weaker pupils, while Brendan Culligan offers very practical advice on teaching the essential if elusive art of spelling, based on his recently published book.

Writing is a far more abstract activity than speaking or reading, and one which makes its own kinds of demand. Jim

Kavanagh's research findings are not reassuring on the health of the teaching of writing in our primary schools. As his research shows, the teaching of writing requires the mastery of writing skills which teachers themselves need to have mastered beforehand. Robert Mohr takes a very practical approach to teaching the more technical if frequently neglected linguistic structures, based in turn on his recent publication. John Devitt's reverie on correcting Leaving Certificate essays provides the basis for his very readable discourse on shortfalls in pupils' learning of essay writing – his essay models its subject.

Curriculum development is a relatively young art on the education scene. The theories and practices informing curricular revision by the National Council for Curriculum and Assessment are ably analysed by Tom Mullins and Pat Coffey with important background information filled in. Understanding the principles that underpin a curriculum ought to give teachers greater owner-ship of it, and thus limit the damage caused by the sabre-toothed tiger of the exam which lies in wait at the end of the course.

A reader is not someone who can read but someone who does read. Writing for young people in Ireland now is flourishing, if changing, and it will not be the fault of our many impressive living authors if too many children still fail to enjoy leisure reading, as Valerie Coghlan's paper shows. Learning to explore, interpret and use language for meaning comes to us first through story. Hearing, and then reading, the stories of others we come to realise that we all live our lives in narrative, constantly telling ourselves (and perhaps others) our own story; it has been said that we turn our joys into narrative so as to prolong them, we turn our pain into narrative to make it bearable. Besides in child-hood, as Graham Greene said, all books are books of divination; they foretell the future.

Writing in non-standard English such as that of Roddy Doyle is gaining ground. But Gerry Mac Ruairc brings us face to face with some of the dilemmas arising for the teacher in the class-room from local language variations in general. These can neither be ignored nor easily solved. Nevertheless, Brian Cox, Tom Mullins and Pat Coffey also make a lot of sense in their comments on this issue.

Not unrelated to this are Learning Support issues which are discussed for us by Ann Whelan of the Irish Learning Support

Association. Is it possible that the very existence of remedial (now called learning support) teachers is taken by some class teachers as suggesting that they no longer need worry about 'the remedials' – as they are often unthinkingly called – in their classes? This, of course, also raises the issue of whether the withdrawal model of learning support, which has become traditional here, should be phased out and – if so – how the school can provide adequate alternatives. This work needs greater coordination between the learning support teacher and all the others in a school. It seems that whole-school planning of the teaching of all pupils with learning difficulties is the best way forward, especially in the context of a policy of inclusion or integration of such pupils, but still without well developed psychological or local authority service structures to support it. While many schools have been seriously under-resourced for implementing such policies in the past, there is now more ground for optimism arising out of the guarantees in the Education Act, 1998.

The findings given in Mark Morgan's article about the extent of adult literacy problems, though testifying to the mounting literacy demands for survival at every level of our society, also warn us against any complacency. At the same time Morgan rightly cautions against interpreting such cross-national comparisons too literally, a footnote frequently overlooked by journalists among others. We are, after all, a singular people living, learning and using language within a particular and specific context.

Lastly the paper by Annette Brady, Ursula Coleman and Rosamond Phillips of the National Adult Literacy Agency testifies to the unique validity and vigour of this area of education, and the serious need for full-scale professional training for workers in this difficult but rewarding field.

The learning of language is central to each person's individual negotiation of meaning. If it fails to bring him or her up to the appropriate levels in listening, speaking, reading, writing, and comprehending themselves and their world, it leaves them dangerously adrift in a world where meaning is paramount. If they do not master their language, they will be at the mercy of the language of others.

The gathering at which the papers that form the core of this book were initially presented was the First National Conference on the Teaching and Usage of English. If their readers benefit as much from reading them as the participants clearly did from engaging with them *in vivo*, their teaching of English will be enhanced and the aims of the organisers, presenters, editors and publishers will be achieved.

For the Editors,
Desmond Swan,
Emeritus Professor of Education,
University College Dublin.
May 1999

References

Crystal, D. (1997) *The Cambridge Encyclopaedia of the English Language*, Cambridge: Cambridge University Press.

Part 1

The tasks and politics of English teaching

1

The multiple tasks of the teacher of English
Kevin Williams

The subject 'English' is complex and multi-faceted and it is important to unravel the different strands of the subject in order to identify the multiple tasks faced by the teacher of English. But firstly it is useful to set these tasks in their historical context.

Understanding the background

Historically language and literature have held a central place in the school curriculum. Western educators were predominantly concerned with the literature and languages of Greece and Rome and only from the time of the Reformation with translations of the Bible did the vernacular begin to assume significance in education. The advent of universal education in the nineteenth century heralded a concern with literacy in vernacular languages. Literature, conceived primarily as a repository of linguistic models rather than as a powerfully sustaining source of personal enrichment, became an important vehicle to this end. Until this century, from the point of view of character formation, classical literature still held sway as a source of moral example to young people. The second half of the century has seen the widespread introduction of vernacular literature on the curriculum. Ironically for almost fifty years after the foundation of the Irish state, the English syllabus in schools was dominated by literature which reflected a very British cultural heritage.

A special tension arises in Ireland regarding the relative status of the English and Irish languages. Irish is the native language of the country but English is the mother tongue of the majority of its citizens. The majority vernacular is also the universal or global language of our times – which is a source of frustration to many English-speakers as they endeavour to find an opportunity to practise their foreign language skills in a world intent on learning English.

Specifying the tasks

There are several tasks involved in teaching the subject 'English' today.[1]

- Developing the skills of written and oral expression. This might be called the technical dimension.

- Teaching literature. We might call this the enrichment dimension.

- Teaching creative writing or the creative dimension.

There is no incompatibility between these different aims and there is enormous overlap between them. Yet there can also be tension. Meeting the demands of the different aspects of the subject represents a great challenge for teachers. Moreover, aspects of the subject 'English' arise across the whole curriculum. Teachers of most subjects require pupils to develop literacy skills and this means that responsibility for developing these skills does not rest *solely* with the English teacher. Today imaginative literature can also be used in Social, Personal and Health Education (SPHE), Relationships and Sexuality Education (RSE), Civic Education, Religious Education, and these and other subjects (History and Geography, for example) may also involve some creative writing. Yet for all the pervasiveness of English throughout the curriculum, teaching literacy, literature and creative writing will always remain the *primary* responsibility of the English teacher.

In Ireland, the teaching of English has been dominated by literary study in the fairly formal sense of literary criticism. Such emphasis detracts from developing functional language skills, from the enrichment potential of literature, and from teaching creative writing. The rest of this chapter will comment on these three aspects of teaching English.

The technical dimension: developing literacy

There is an irony in the evidence from employers which calls into question the effectiveness of the school in developing ability at the skill which is its dominant concern, that is, discursive writing. In an extensive survey, not a single employer rated the skills of written communication of their employees as excellent and only 10 per cent rated them as very good. (More positively it should be noted that 40 per cent rated these skills as good, 42 per cent as fair and only seven per cent as poor.[2]) On this matter it is easy to romanticise the past through an exaggerated view of the quality of the writing skills of previous generations. After all, in the mid-1960s less than one-fifth of the age cohort sat the Leaving Certificate compared to approximately four-fifths today. I am also sceptical of the claim that the reduction in numbers studying Latin has been a significant contributor to an alleged decline in standards of written English. Admittedly the study of Latin may have enhanced the grammatical sensitivity of some very able students. But until we have detailed and plausible research evidence, it remains mere assertion to maintain that the writing skills of those who studied Latin are better than those who did not. In the last few decades, however, especially at second level, there has been a failure to pay sufficient attention to teaching writing skills or what is called in the USA 'composition'. This is hardly surprising because the professional education of many English teachers has itself been concerned almost exclusively with literature.

How then should we set about improving writing skills?

Developing literacy requires sustained, serious and focused attention to the mechanics of written and oral communication or to what might be called the development of communicative competence. The production of creative, discursive and functional prose needs to be supplemented by the intensive and systematic teaching of grammar, punctuation and spelling, together with work in comprehension and vocabulary enhancement. Contrary to the intuitions of educational romantics with little experience in the classroom, young people often find functional work quite satisfying. This activity gives them the opportunity to complete specific, concrete tasks which tend not to be a feature of literary study. As well as grammar and syntax, we need to engage in a serious attempt to cultivate language awareness. By this I mean a kind of comparative linguistics which would develop in young people a sense of human languages as systems, each with its own peculiar way of representing the world.

Of course, not all communication takes place through the written word. In the development of the other aspects of communicative competence, the dramatic and performing arts have a crucial role to play. It is important for young people to learn how their speech and deportment convey to others an impression of their whole personalities. Good self-presentation is important not only at interviews but also in general social situations. Drama and the performing arts contribute hugely to the improvement of communicative competence and, by extension, to overall personal development. By freeing young people from some of their inhibiting self-consciousness, drama has a unique potential to enhance self-confidence.

The enrichment dimension: the teaching of literature

Literary study has its own internal tension – between the study of literature in a formal, technical sense and the promotion of a very individual engagement with texts with a view to personal enrichment. In teaching literature, excessive emphasis on literary criticism rather than on literature as a source of personal interest, satisfaction and delight is like teaching religion in a purely academic sense without a concern for its potential in faith formation. Yet even where the focus is primarily academic, the study of literature retains its potential to enrich the lives of learners. Literature studies make a special and vital contribution to the development of human self-understanding. In particular, the store of literature which we acquire during our schooldays shapes and informs our imagination and sensibility. What we learn at school can and should contribute in a significant and positive manner to making us the kind of persons we are. What we learn at school also has the potential to offer a world of joy and delight, of captivating excitement, enchantment and wonder.

Nonetheless, the internal tension in literary study has implications for assessment in literature which merits comment. Obviously examinations can create tension with regard to any area of the curriculum, but this tension is particularly acute with regard to the study of literature where creation and response are so rooted in students' personal lives. Students whose responses to literature are most deeply felt do not necessarily provide the most coherent or perceptive analyses of literary works, especially in written examinations where facility at abstract discourse is crucial. Balancing the demands of the detached response which is mainly concerned with matters of technique, form and content and the involved response which refers to the feelings of the person who responds, is a task requiring utmost sensitivity (see Williams, 1995a, 1998a). The foregoing should not to be understood to imply that the presence of assessment takes away the pleasure from the study of literature. Although this can happen, it is hardly inevitable. Human beings tend to act from mixed motives and there will be some tension inherent in any system of formal assessment in literature. But it does not follow that the presence of assessment must compromise the educational value of the study of literature. There is no reason why students studying literature for the Junior Certificate or for the Leaving Certificate examination (or for any other kind of examination) should not also derive pleasure and satisfaction from their study.

Literature across the curriculum

The potential contribution of literature to personal development means that it can play a significant role in personal and social education courses. Literary texts offer a context through which to explore delicate subjects such as sexuality, marriage, addiction, and unemployment in a way which allows the teacher to avoid making direct use of the experience of the pupils themselves. In the phrase of T. S. Eliot's, literature offers an 'objective correlative' (Eliot, 1972: 145), that is, an expression of emotion which exists independently of the pupils' lives and to which they can relate. In this way the teacher can avoid directly drawing on the pupils' own experience as subject-matter in class.

Take, for example, the possible use of literature in dealing with issues of death and bereavement in the classroom. By providing imaginative experience of aspects of the human response to death, the teacher can help young people to an enlarged under-standing of the feelings involved. Those who have suffered the sorrow and pain of bereavement, and those who have yet to experience them, can learn much by sharing vicariously in the feelings articulated in literature, especially in poetry. Poetry can provide an important source of insight and at times of consolation in the face of the mystery and pain of death. A striking feature of many of the poems on the (recently replaced) Leaving Certificate English syllabus is the prominence of the theme of death – indeed the poems chosen could even be said to be excessively preoccupied with death, dying, loss, bereavement, mourning and the transience of life. This is quite obvious if we consider some of the titles of the poems – 'No Longer Mourn for Me When I Am Dead', 'Terror of Death', 'Because I Could Not Stop for Death', 'I Felt a Funeral in My Brain', 'A Refusal to Mourn'.

To provide young people with the experience of a poem, the teacher does not have to convert every line of the poem into prose. In fact, the attempt to translate poetry into other words can destroy what is most significant in poetic expression. For example, the complex and allusive language of Dylan Thomas's 'A Refusal to Mourn' does not lend itself to prose paraphrase. Yet the poem, which deals with the theme of youthful death, has a power and energy which is capable of speaking to everyone, and its last line, 'after the first death, there is no other', is perfectly accessible. We must not underestimate the capacity of young people to respond to the rhythm, mood and images of a poem even if the language is complex. Although, for example, the language of John Milton's great poem, 'Lycidas', would be found difficult by some pupils, this should not prevent the teacher from taking extracts from the poem. Lines such as 'for Lycidas is dead, dead ere his prime/ Young Lycidas . . . hath not left his peer:/Who would not sing for Lycidas' can be readily understood. The sorrow expressed by the poet over the death of his young friend and contemporary is in fact no different from that in the poignant lament, 'Old Pal', composed by Brush Shields in memory of rock musician, Phil Lynott. Both poet and songwriter are lamenting the untimely deaths of young men of creative talent. Another poem which will also move young readers is Wordsworth's 'Surprised by Joy'. In telling the confused tumult of his grief that the loss of his daughter can never be made good, Wordsworth's is the voice of humankind itself.

Expressing different human responses to dying, death, bereavement and grieving many of the poems in the Leaving Certificate anthology could well be included as part of a unit in Social, Personal and Health Education (SPHE) or in Religious Education (see O'Sullivan et al., 1993). Using literature for pastoral purposes is, however, somewhat different from the traditional teaching of literature in English class. In the pastoral context, the emphasis is primarily on the contribution of literature to the education of understanding and feeling rather than on its formal features as literary art. Yet obviously literature retains the potential to help young people to understand human emotion in whatever context it is taught.

Teaching literature with a direct pastoral intent has given rise to concern on the part of some teachers that literary texts will be treated as mere moral tracts. The fear that literature may be reduced to a source of material for personal and social and moral education is understandable. Literature, however, always teaches us about life and so every work of literature could be said to be didactic. (One characteristic of some bad literature is that it is merely didactic.) Likewise, through teaching literature we always come to teach something about life, although teaching about life in a narrow, didactic manner is not the purpose of teaching literature. Much will depend how the literature is *mise en scène* or presented. Teachers must display the pedagogic tact necessary to avoid an instrumental and reductionist approach and to ensure that the encounters which young people have with literature are sensitive to the complexity of literary works. Helping student teachers to learn this tact is a matter for teacher educators.

Responding to literature must be supplemented by an opportunity to write creatively and I shall conclude with some remarks on the place of creative writing in the teaching of English.

Who will read my stories?

Creative writing needs to retain a place throughout all of the school years both because it is a fulfilling activity in itself and also because it contributes enormously to the development of communicative competence. In *The Woman Who Walked into Doors* by Roddy Doyle, Paula O'Leary/Spencer's treasured memories of her primary school days capture very dramatically the educational potential of creative writing.

> I was good in school, especially at stories. [The teacher] always got me to read mine out to the class . . . I loved that . . . . I remember the applause after and the smiles. I was good in school; she made us think that we were good. (Doyle, 1996: 25)

Her encounter with second-level schooling was very different. Through Paula, Doyle expresses the disappointment that must be shared by other young people as their English lessons take them further away from the story writing of primary school.

The young person's own experience can often lie at the core of their creative writing in a way that does not occur, for example, in the study of physics or of accountancy. The student's own experience assumes a centrality here which occurs elsewhere only in religious education (see Williams, 1998b). When I left second-level teaching in the early 1980s I was confronted by a very angry young man about to start sixth year. To my discomfiture, he berated me for abandoning him. 'When you are gone', he bitterly exclaimed, 'who will read my stories?' The young man had become used to pouring out the pain of his life in the stories that he managed to make of even the most abstract and discursive of essay titles. Every teacher of English, as reader of such stories, often encounters the very quick of students' experience. It is an awesome and humbling privilege.

Notes

1 For the purposes of this chapter, the possible role of such areas as Media Studies and Film Studies is not examined.
2 See Confederation of Irish Industry (1990) for the source of these findings. Detailed analysis of the survey can be found in Williams (1994 and 1995b). In chapter 15 of this volume, Mark Morgan provides further evidence regarding literacy skills in Ireland

References

Confederation of Irish Industry (1990), 'Human resources – the key issues.' *CII Newsletter*, 53(9): 1–7.

Doyle, R. (1996) *The Woman Who Walked into Doors*, London: Jonathan Cape.

Eliot, T.S. (1972), *Selected Essays*, London: Faber & Faber.

O'Sullivan, M. et al. (1993) 'Death and bereavement in the school curriculum.' In: Donal Harrington (ed.), *Death and New Life: Pastoral and Theological Reflections*, Dublin: Dominican Publications.

Williams, K. (1994) 'Vocationalism and liberal education'. *Journal of Philosophy of Education*, 28(1): 89–100.

Williams, K. (1995a) 'Review article: Are we too defensive about the place of the arts in education?'*Journal of Philosophy of Education*, 29(1): 149–54.

Williams, K. (1995b) 'Philosophy and curriculum policy.' In: Pádraig Hogan (ed.), *Partnership and the Benefits of Learning: A Symposium on Philosophical Issues in Educational Policy*, Maynooth: Educational Studies Association of Ireland.

Williams, K. (1998a) 'Assessment and the challenge of scepticism.' In: David Carr (ed.) *Knowledge, Truth and Education: Beyond the Postmodern Impasse*, London/New York: Routledge.

Williams, K. (1998b) 'Religion, culture and schooling.' In: J. Matthew Feheny (ed.), *From Ideal to Action: The Inner Nature of a Catholic School Today*, Dublin: Veritas.

2

Controversies in Britain over a National Curriculum in English

Brian Cox

Sir John Kingman chaired the British Committee of Inquiry into the Teaching of English Language which reported in 1988. When in the same year I was asked to chair the National Curriculum English Working Group he wrote to me that he was passing on to me a poisoned chalice. He did not exaggerate.

A National Curriculum in English raises highly sensitive questions about national identity and personal identity. Well-educated older people may be asked to reconsider whether their much-cherished ideas about the teaching of English are true, and whether the material they studied is appropriate to the modern age. They may be told that the books they loved as a child are racist or that the rules they have enforced on their children – that you must never split the infinitive, for example – are wrong. The newspapers will almost certainly simplify issues, and look greedily for stories about the folly of whoever – like me – tries to lay down standards for a National Curriculum in English.

In my case, personal attacks began as soon as my Working Group published its first Report on schooling for primary school children. I did not want to publish a report that consisted only of abstractions and generalisations, so I included references to books to enliven our pages. In a list of recommended authors we did not include Enid Blyton and Captain W. E. Johns, author of the Biggles stories. As you will know, some teachers think these two authors are racist, and some find Enid Blyton's use of language banal. The tabloids attacked me as the man who had put his knife into Noddy and his boot into Biggles.

The teaching of grammar also caused us many problems with the press. On the day our Report was published, two newspapers reacted with completely contradictory headlines. One headline said 'Back to Basics' and continued: 'The academic debate over free expression versus rigid rules in the teaching of English has been raging for almost 20 years, to the detriment of a generation of schoolchildren. Now Mr Kenneth Baker [then the Secretary of State] is determined to return to old-fashioned methods of teaching grammar.' On the same day another newspaper headline read: 'Baker accepts defeat on teaching of grammar' and then continued: 'Mr Kenneth Baker, the Education Secretary, yesterday conceded that the government cannot force schools to adopt his preference for formal grammar teaching.' (Cox, 1991) Our recommendation that grammar should be taught, but through language in use, not by the learning off by heart of rigid definitions, naturally confused more simple-minded journalists.

Establishing a national curriculum: the issue of grammar

My discussion of the problems in establishing a National Curriculum will start by considering the great debates about the teaching of grammar. When I was at school in the 1930s and 1940s English was often taught badly. After the outbreak of war in 1939 the Army found that many conscripts were illiterate, and could not read firearm and safety instructions. In those years children were taught rules about the English language which are now recognised as false. A teacher in his sixties told me that when he was at school he was cuffed for writing 'a dilapidated wooden shed'. 'Lapis means a stone' proclaimed his teacher, tweaking his ear. 'You foolish boy, you can't call something wooden dilapidated.' As late as the 1960s a professor at Bedford College, London, told his students that 'companion' must only be used for a person with whom one eats ('panis' means 'with bread, food'). These teachers were applying Latin rules to English, and we now realise that this is ridiculous. Children were taught not to begin sentences with 'and' or 'but', and not to end a sentence with a preposition. My teacher in primary school, with a twinkle in his eye, told us: 'Never end a sentence with *with*.' Children were told not to split the infinitive. In my early years as a teacher I always corrected essays where students had split the infinitive. For some time now linguists have been demonstrating that these rules do not apply to the English language, particularly to its spoken forms.

Lay people often believe that grammatical exercises should be imposed on all pupils, and that this would improve standards of writing. It depends what kinds of grammatical exercises are involved. When I was at school we spent a great deal of time learning clause analysis, and I found this precise and easy to handle. A friend of mine who taught in a grammar school in an inner city told me that the children in the lower forms could comparatively easily be taught how to analyse clauses, and this could help them to pass the old School Certificate, for which English Language was compulsory. However, he also found that they forgot clause analysis very quickly, and that it had little or no influence on their ability to use English clearly and forcibly. His opinions have been validated by several high profile pieces of research. Among the most important was a New Zealand study carried out between 1970 and 1973. The language growth of 248 pupils in eight matched classes from a large suburban co-educational high school was monitored over three years. One group studied a traditional grammar course, one a transformational grammar course and the third had no grammar teaching at all. Reviewing the evidence at the end of the three years, the researchers concluded that 'it is difficult to escape the conclusion that English grammar, whether traditional or transformational, has virtually no influence of the language growth of typical secondary school students.' (Elley et al., 1975).

In Britain in the 1950s and 1960s, good teachers, dissatisfied with what they saw as the sterile teaching of grammar, often completely abandoned the teaching of grammar. Indeed, the new British Government guidelines for the teaching of English grammar accept that many trainee teachers will have almost no knowledge of grammar. In the 1960s the pendulum swung too far.

Because grammar had been taught badly, no grammar was taught. 'Creative' writing became fashionable, and in some classrooms children were encouraged to express themselves freely without bothering about spelling, punctuation and grammar.

The National English Curriculum of 1989 strongly opposed this trend, and recommended carefully structured programmes of work based on language in use. We emphasised that high quality in the use of language is a disciplined craft. We urged that grammatical terminology should be introduced as a common vocabulary for teachers and pupils to discuss their own writing. This is the strongest argument for the teaching of grammatical terminology. When teachers are discussing a draft piece of prose with a pupil they need a vocabulary with which to discuss the writing. (And while I recognise that the old lessons on grammar were often of little value, I believe that the old exercises in précis writing were of real value. To prepare a précis is an activity which is common in normal business life, and which we need to perform regularly when we are communicating with other people.)

Knowledge about language

In the 1989 National Curriculum we proposed what we saw as exciting programmes for the teaching of knowledge about language in Britain. It is easy to persuade children to be fascinated by language. They can be asked to compare their usage with that of their grandparents. For example, now I am in my late sixties I might say: 'I motored to the aerodrome with my wife listening to the wireless.' Three words here – 'motored', 'aerodrome' and 'wireless' – are no longer in common usage among young people. Once when I used this example in a lecture an undergraduate pointed out to me that 'wife' too is out of date. I should have said 'partner'. From this interest in language shifts children can, I believe, be persuaded to look at changes in grammar. In my day the formal teaching of grammar referred to the systematic instruction in the analysis of sentences. It was systematic in that it was deliberately designed to help pupils break down sentences into their component parts. It included instruction on the labelling of sentence components – subject and predicate, phrases, clauses, word classes (nouns, verbs, prepositions) and their use in breaking down, building and editing sentences. The problem with this kind of grammar teaching is that it was dull, and that the definitions were often not wholly true.

One aim of the 1989 National Curriculum for English was to find methods in which grammar could be taught so that it would excite and fascinate children. Knowledge about language was seen as a useful means of beginning to accomplish this.

Beyond 'functional' literacy

Grammar, of course, means different things to different people. In everyday usage and in the newspapers, 'grammar' is associated with the correct use of the standard language. The word 'correct' raises many problems, and I shall return to these. Linguists use the term 'grammar', first, to refer to ways in which words are combined to make sentences (in any dialect), and second, to label the body of statements they write about the language as they attempt to make explicit the implicit knowledge possessed by all native speakers of English.

Many people still believe that English grammar is a fixed form, stable and unchanging, which obeys logical rules. When the 1989 National Curriculum Report was published it received a scathing review in the London *Evening Standard* from John Rae, previously head of Westminster School in London. He wrote:

> I thought it was correct to write we were and incorrect to write *we was*. I did not realise it was just a question of dialect; I thought it was a question of grammar or, if you do not like that word, of logic. You cannot use a singular form of the verb with a plural pronoun. (17 November, 1988)

The arrogance of this review, written by a typical public school headmaster of the old school, demonstrates the ignorance about language common among many highly educated people. It demonstrates the urgent need for a National Curriculum which includes a carefully organised section on knowledge about language. Rae's appeal to logic is so obviously mistaken. 'You were' is both singular and plural in Standard English. Logic is a feature not of the grammar of a language or dialect, but of arguments in sentences and in texts. It is people in their use of language who are logical or illogical, not languages or dialects themselves.

The National Curriculum of 1989 recommends that dialects should be respected, but that by the end of their schooling all children should be able to speak and write Standard English. May I stress here that my Committee made no recommendation that Received Pronunciation should be enforced. As long as their accent does not prevent communication, children should be proud of their regional accents.

For the teacher it is important to understand the difference between a local dialect usage and a mistake. A teacher who is not local might well reprove a child for a usage which is part of his or her local dialect. The teacher's attitude to such usage should be very different from what happens when the child makes a mistake. To correct dialect is a matter of sensitivity and tact; it is not wise to tell a child that his or her mother uses English incorrectly. The child needs to understand that there are two ways of saying things, a dialect and the Standard. Children will be introduced to Standard English in writing as soon as they can read; when to introduce Standard English in speech is much more controversial.

Some teachers believe it can be done by the age of eight or nine; others think that it should wait until children are twelve or thirteen when they might want to speak Standard English and realise why it is important. I have no sympathy for those who believe children should be left to speak their own dialects and not introduced to Standard English. Standard English is the language of higher education and of politics. To leave children without this ability is to condemn them to the ghetto. Standard English is the main international language, and it is vital that the various Standards – American, Australian and so on – should never diverge so far that we cannot all understand the one language.

I recently edited a book to be published at the start of the year of reading by the Book Trust. It is called *Literacy Is Not Enough*, and contributors include Richard Hoggart, Doris Lessing and Antonia Byatt. Our main point is that there is probably no such thing as functional literacy. Literacy develops in a critical, imaginative and creative context when children are excited and find pleasure in reading. Literacy is very much a matter of actual experience in the production and reception of texts. The danger of 'back to basics' campaigns is that they reduce language to abstract formulas and to sterile exercises. So while I approve of my Government's emphasis on literacy, I am deeply critical of the reduction of literacy to the learning of rules. Children must want to express themselves, to enjoy communication; otherwise they will never develop their true potential.

Language: change and convention

This still leaves me with the huge problem of defining what is 'correct'. We know that language changes quite rapidly. Because of more liberal attitudes to race, today we would never use the word 'nigger' or 'coon'. Women very properly object when 'he' is used as a generic pronoun. A sensible politician always says 'he or she'. Only thirty years ago this was not common. Feminism has brought about changes in language, so that I now call myself a Chair because I know the term 'chairman' may annoy women. Public school speakers who have visited the United States have been heckled when they have used 'boys' to cover both sexes in the schools.

But if language is changing how do we tell a child what is correct and incorrect?

In his recent book, *Language is Power: The Story of Standard English and its Enemies* (1997) John Honey argues for an official academy to prescribe usage. I think this is impractical because language has a life of its own and will not obey academicians. But we do need authoritative text-books to clarify this difficult question of 'correct' conventional usage. The last thing we want is the doctrine that anything goes.

For example, is 'a government' or 'a board' singular or plural? I was taught that they are singular, but many educated speakers now use the plural. How many people today understand the difference between 'owing to' and 'due to'? Does it matter? I would argue that it does and that such distinctions are of immense importance if we are to maintain the highest standards of clarity and accuracy.

As words shift in meaning and rules are broken, teachers face a formidable task. Conservatives want an ordered, fixed, authoritative system to be imposed on all children. Non-conformists, and this category includes many great writers, want to use language in new and exciting ways. This issue brings out how much the teaching of English is an art, a matter of relating to specific children in specific contexts, rather than a set of rules. There needs to be a careful balance between prescription and description. Linguists may not like prescriptions, but in school they are inevitable. I am strongly in favour of a National Curriculum, but there is always a danger that its prescriptions will interfere with good teaching. A National Curriculum must reflect good practice in the schools, and must allow a large degree of flexibility for the individual teacher.

The teaching of English is of great importance in the quest for identity, both personal and national, because speaking, reading and writing provide roads to freedom, freedom from political control, freedom for the consciousness to pick and choose among competing value systems. My views on this are influenced by the writing of the Cambridge linguist, Sylvia Adamson. She shows how, for the structuralists of the 1970s, language was seen as a static, self-sustaining system, a tracery of prepared forms from which there is no escape. The language system determined all thought and expression; it is a prison-house whose inhabitants are deprived of free speech. Sylvia Adamson argues that in Saussure's distinction between *langue* and *parole*, whereas the language system is passively assimilated by the individual, speaking (*parole*) is an individual act. It is in speaking that the germ of all change is found. Every child is free in speech to create its own meanings, its own unique voice. Adamson discusses what might be deemed the paradox of the passive yet innovative speaker. She writes:

> The paradox appears not as a problem but as a solution. The solution depends on the existence of two kinds of meaning – on the one hand, meanings that are encoded in the vocabulary and grammar of the language and, on the other, meanings that arise contingently and by improvisation in particular contexts of speaking. (Adamson, 1990)

So language as activity begins to impress itself upon language as a system, changing the code to accommodate the needs of its speakers.

From this point of view the teaching of drama, with active participation in role-play and the production of plays, is of major importance in developing high standards of speech. We live in a society where speech is of increasing importance. We do not want young people who have spent their school careers in passive assimilation of facts.

These distinctions are – in my view – central to the teaching of language in a National Curriculum. Children need to assimilate meanings encoded in the vocabulary and grammar of the language; at the same time they need to explore their own meanings that arise contingently and by improvisation in particular contexts of speaking. Both elements are crucial. This is why I suggested that the notion of functional literacy can become repressive. We need balance between the learning of what is correct, the rules, and freedom to develop with pleasure and confidence one's own meanings.

Literature: the heart of literacy

I believe the teaching of literature must be at the heart of all successful teaching of language. In our responses to the English language, both as readers and writers, we depend on an intimate feeling for words and rhythms and innuendoes and images and ironies that can only be achieved by exposure to great English literature.

The Kingman Report catches well the sense of this and is worth quoting at length:

> Wide reading, and as great an experience as possible of the best imaginative literature, are essential to the full development of an ear for language, and to a full knowledge of the range of possible patterns of thought and feeling made accessible by the power and range of language. Matching book to the pupil is an aspect of the English teacher's work which requires fine judgement and sensitivity to the needs of the child. It is good for children to respond to good contemporary works, written both for children and for adults. It is equally important for them to read and hear and speak the great literature of the past. Our modern language and our modern writing have grown out of the language and literature of the past. The rhythms of our daily speech and writing are haunted not only by the rhythms of nursery rhymes, but also by the rhythms of Shakespeare, Blake, Edward Lear, Lewis Carroll, the Authorised Version of the Bible. We do not completely know what modern writing is unless we know what lies behind it. Hemingway's short sentences derive their power from their revolt against earlier, more discursive styles. *The Diary of Adrian Mole* is a descendant of Dickens's urgent, knowingly innocent style. The apparently 'free' verse of D.H. Lawrence is imbued with the rhythms of the Book of Common Prayer.

And Kingman continues in the next paragraph:

> It is possible that a generation of children may grow up deprived of their entitlement – an introduction to the powerful and splendid history of the best that has been thought and said in our language. Too rigid a concern with what is 'relevant' to the lives of young people seems to us to pose the danger of impoverishing not only the young people, but the culture itself, which has to be revitalised by each generation. (Kingman, 1988)

I believe that the implicit relativism which crept into much cultural analysis in the 1970s and 1980s is already past its peak, and that these traditional words, heavily dependent on Matthew Arnold, are reclaiming their proper authority. There is an increasing insistence on 'quality'. As Harold Bloom wrote in his book, *The Western Canon*:

> One breaks into the canon only by aesthetic strength, which is constituted primarily of an amalgam: mastery of figurative language, originality, cognitive power, knowledge, exuberance of diction. (Bloom, 1995)

A knowledge of literature gives pupils a whole series of literary associations such as names, quotations, and other references which are part of the cultural inheritance of people in the English speaking world. Some of these literary elements are part of the language and have their place in standard dictionaries: others are quasi-proverbial and often used without an awareness of their origin. The effect is not confined to works composed in English. Aesop's Fables and H.C. Andersen's stories plus translated works such as classical stories from Greece and Rome often appear in references. The value of this background is not just the ability to spot literary references. It provides a basis for fuller understanding of allusion, implication and inference. It also involves an introduction to forms of discourse that were powerful in the past and from which our own culture has developed. They are an integral part of the living language.

It is said that the literary work most often quoted in the British House of Commons is *Alice in Wonderland* – 'jam yesterday, jam tomorrow but never jam today'. Other literary allusions such as to Hamlet's delay, Oliver Twist's asking for more, or Micawberism can only be understood by pupils with a good reading background.

My Working Group eventually decided that in the secondary school Shakespeare must figure in all syllabuses, but that teachers should be given some freedom in their choice of plays. We recommended no other specific author but put forward the following three recommendations about the books appropriate for study in the secondary school:

(a) they must be taken from a variety of genres;

(b) pupils need to be aware of the richness of contemporary writing, but they should also be introduced to pre-twentieth-century literature. We felt that teachers should introduce pupils to some of the works which have been most influential in shaping and refining the English language and its literature – for example, the Authorised Version of the Bible, Wordsworth's poems, or Dickens's novels. When the final report was published we added Jane Austen and the Brontës to this list;

(c) pupils should encounter and find pleasure in literary works written in English – particularly new works – from different parts of the world.

I am very much opposed to the inclusion of lists of books in National Curriculum Statutory Orders. If a list of set texts is published, their names become engraved in stone and the canon becomes unchangeable, reflecting out-of-date literary and social opinions. When I was at school in the 1930s and 1940s the canon would have included Kinglake's *Eothen*, Thomas Hughes's *Tom Brown's Schooldays*, Charles Kingsley's *The Water Babies* and the essays of Charles Lamb, all little read by the young today. The American critic Robert Scholes insists that the establishment of a canon, a list of great masterpieces, works of genius, removes the chosen texts from history and human actualities, placing them for ever behind a veil of pieties; it fosters a reverential rather than a critical approach. This explains the bardolatry that has dominated so much writing about Shakespeare.

The great danger of a National Curriculum for English is that it might impose the dead hand of received opinions on the schools, and not allow innovation and experiment. Shakespeare is a highly subversive writer. His sonnets, for example, express strongly homoerotic feelings. Should such elements never be mentioned to bright sixth-formers? Shakespeare often failed to bother with full stops and probably never used the question mark. Children need to be encouraged to write for themselves. They need to learn the rules, to know how to write clear, accurate English. On the other hand they must not be turned into robots, obeying slavishly a series of conventions.

There is also the danger of censorship. When in 1993 the Conservative Party published lists of modern writers to be read in schools they missed out Tony Harrison, in my view the poet whose recent work is the most powerful among writers from England. He has his great poem, 'V', on television. Tony Harrison, of course, is well known for his anti-Conservative writings.

Texts to be studied must include some works in English from other cultures. The most dynamic English today is often found outside England and indeed outside Ireland: from Saul Bellow, Alice Walker and Toni Morrison from the United States, Anita Desai from India, Nadine Gordimer from South Africa, V.S. Naipaul from Trinidad, Chinua Achebe from Nigeria, for example. All pupils need to be aware of the richness of experience offered by writing in English from different countries, so that they can be introduced to the ideas and feelings of countries different from their own, and so we shall help the cause of racial tolerance. As we all move closer to Europe and as the world becomes – by air travel – so much more accessible, we need to adopt this world-view to texts. A concern for our own national literary heritage needs to be balanced with an openness to literature from a great variety of cultures.

Throughout my career, teachers of English have believed passionately that enjoyment of great literature is intimately involved with the development of the moral life. This is not the place to look in detail at the controversies that have surrounded this belief, particularly with regard to the dogmas of F. R. Leavis. Instead, I quote a few sayings which sum up my own view of the supreme importance of reading and literature. In *The Western Canon* Harold Bloom writes: 'Aesthetic criticism returns us to the autonomy of imaginative literature and the sovereignty of the solitary soul, the reader not as a person in society but as the deep self, our ultimate inwardness.' (Bloom, 1995.) In *The Gutenberg Elegies* Sven Birkerts writes: 'What reading does, ultimately, is keep alive the dangerous and exhilarating idea that a life is not a sequence of lived moments, but a destiny.' He also says: '. . .

serious reading is above all an agency of self-making' (Birkerts, 1994). The poet Joseph Brodsky in his 1987 Nobel Prize acceptance speech said: 'If art teaches anything . . . it is the privateness of the human condition. Being the most ancient as well as the most literal form of private enterprise, it fosters in a man, knowingly or unwittingly, a sense of his uniqueness, of individuality, of separateness – thus turning him from a social animal into an autonomous "I".' (In Birkerts, 1994.) And Birkerts again: 'The novel will not endure because it can entertain (although certainly it can) but because it offers an essential experience available nowhere else.' (Birkerts, 1994)

Literature and media studies

I ought perhaps to say a word here about media studies. After the 1989 National Curriculum was published, it was criticised by Colin MacCabe, from the British Film Institute, who argued that literature was declining in its influence on the public. Radio, film, video and television have become the dominant art forms in a democratic society, and they unite us all; therefore they should be at the centre of the curriculum. English teachers, he argued, are deluded if they think the main significance of media studies is their usefulness for English, if they think that the value of soaps is only that they help us to study Dickens's use of the serial, or that the principal educational importance of seeing *Pride and Prejudice* on television is that pupils might be helped to read and enjoy the novel. Children are fascinated by films and TV. Many programmes are of the highest quality, great art, and they should be studied in the classroom.

This is a debate which must continue: I do not have glib solutions.

I still believe that reading, the isolated individual lost in a book, is of central importance in a democratic society. I do not think there is any evidence that reading is in decline. Indeed there is evidence that more titles are published than ever before and that the readership for good novels is increasing. Above all, literature is an honest attempt to use words to purvey the truth. I believe it should remain at the heart of the English curriculum.

Control of content

Who should control a National Curriculum in English?

My experiences in England have taught me the hard way how important this question is, and how dangerous it can be to allow power to fall into the wrong hands. The teaching of language can induce passivity or encourage a critical spirit. Choices of books for study have political implications, as I have shown. Indeed, political intervention of the most ill-judged kind can result from power resting with the wrong people.

For example, after the National Curriculum was published in 1989 a major attempt was made to help teachers to develop knowledge about language. This was called LINC; Language in the National Curriculum. It was very successful, but after three years it was stopped by the Conservative Government. Why? Because of political pressure from extremists on the right wing of the Party, and because the scheme was attacked by the tabloid newspapers. The Secretary of State, Kenneth Clarke, was anxious to improve his standing among the right wing of the Party, and this was an important element in the decision to stop funding LINC.

I would normally say that control of the curriculum should be in the hands of the professionals. In England I have often argued for a General Teaching Council with power over the curriculum. I believe such a Council should have representatives nominated by different sectors of the education world – nursery schools, primary schools, secondary schools, heads, the universities, special schools – and that membership should not be controlled by politicians. Such a proposal goes completely against what has become common practice in England from both the Conservative Party and now our new Labour Government. This would seem to me to be a great pity.

In my dealings with politicians I have found that they are far too much influenced by popular newspapers. The body in charge of a National Curriculum may need to take decisions in the interests of children which create bad publicity in the tabloid press, or which may be misrepresented for political reasons. A National Curriculum must represent all that is best in classroom teaching. In England in 1992 the Education Minister, John Patten, allowed a very small group of extreme right-wing people to take control of the curriculum. In 1993 he was faced with a teachers' boycott of national tests. The situation has improved since then, but the resulting confusions from the right-wing interference of 1992 to 1993 have left us with a curriculum in English which is unexciting and which does not attract the support of the best teachers.

The argument against control by professionals is that in the 1960s and 1970s teachers allowed themselves to be brainwashed by an extreme progressivism which still damages the quality of some teachers trained during this period. From this point of view, the general public, through its parliamentary representatives, should retain final control.

I believe these two positions can be reconciled. The events of the 1960s and 1970s were exceptional. For the last 15 years or so there has been a general consensus about how to combine the best of formal and informal methods of teaching. Obviously, there must always be disagreement about the best methods of teaching, but a National Curriculum can be devised which allows good teachers flexibility. Teachers succeed by various methods and no government should force good teachers to adopt ways of teaching which do not fit their style and commitments. How to assess a national curriculum is another highly contentious question. I recommend a proper balance between course assessment and formal examinations.

Governments should judge teachers by their success in maintaining standards. Only when there is a palpable decline in standards should a government interfere. I favour an arrangement rather like that which operates for the Arts Council in England – an arm's length principle which allows professionals to control the curriculum as long as they have general public support.

I believe very strongly in the importance of a National Curriculum, in spite of our English problems. Teaching is an exhausting activity, and it is so easy for teachers as the years go by to repeat what they found successful when young and charismatic. Teachers have full programmes of work, and often little contact with other teachers in their discipline. After the introduction of the National Curriculum in English a great benefit was that teachers in a school had to cooperate together to create appropriate programmes of work, and that course assessment arrangements forced teachers in one area to meet each other and to discuss their work. A National Curriculum also makes possible comparisons between schools, between success and failure, and this has led to energetic attempts in England to reform failing schools.

The achievement of high standards in education is today more important than ever before. As technology takes over so many processes previously demanding manual labour we need educated young people who can adapt quickly to changing conditions. For this purpose high standards in English are vital. We need people who can think and write lucidly and accurately. The critical spirit inculcated by a proper study of literature is of crucial importance. Let me finish with a final quotation from Birkerts (1994): '. . . language is the soul's ozone layer, and we thin it at our peril'.

References

Adamson, S. (1990) 'The what of the language?' In: Ricks, C. and L. Michaels (eds), *The State of the Language*, London: Faber & Faber.

Birkerts, S. (1994) *The Gutenberg Galaxies*, London: Faber & Faber.

Bloom, H. (1995) *The Western Canon*, London: Macmillan.

Cox, B. (1991) *Cox on Cox: An English Curriculum for the 1990s*, London: Hodder & Stoughton.

Elley, W.B., et al. (1975) 'The role of grammar in a secondary school curriculum.' *New Zealand Journal of Educational Studies*, Vol. 10: 26–42.

Kingman, J. (1988) *Report of the Committee of Inquiry into the Teaching of English Language*, London: HMSO.

3

Grounds for hope:
a response to Brian Cox
Declan Kiberd

W.B. Yeats said that the nation was the gloved hand with which people reach out to possess and hold a world (see Reynolds, 1934/1970: 174) – and I would agree. At the very least, the nation provides a point of departure. Later, any thinker worthy of the name will want to refine or even explode the original national idea, but it remains a force to be reckoned with all the same. It may at times seem an imposition to be expected to answer to a definite gender, or age, or nationality, but even those who question such notions tend to answer the relevant questions about such matters on passports. Besides, one can increasingly do this with a certain irony – as when the writer Dermot Bolger chose to place a photo of Marilyn Monroe on the cover of his Picador book of contemporary Irish prose. Doubtless, many of the authors in that collection would have endorsed Flaubert's claim that 'Bohemia is my native country' or even John Banville's refusal to write from within the stable entity called Irish culture. But even Banville does not appear to object when his books are filed in shops under the label 'Irish Writing'. Nor should he take umbrage, for even in his flaunted indifference to his Irishness he is noticing the national narrative, managing, like Joyce before him to be anti-Irish in a very Irish way. Once, when asked how he had so unerringly managed to recreate the late medieval world of witches, alchemists and spells in his science trilogy, Banville answered: 'Oh, that was easy – I grew up in Wexford in the 1950s'.

For these reasons, and many more, I think that the concept of a national curriculum is to be lauded, not just defended. Yet the case against certain forms of national curriculum is a very old one: at the start of this century, for instance, Patrick Pearse found it upsetting to think that:

> . . . precisely the same textbooks are being read tonight in every secondary school in Ireland. Two of Hawthorne's *Tanglewood Tales*, with a few poems in English, will constitute the whole literary pabulum of three-quarters of the pupils of the Irish secondary schools during this twelvemonth. The teacher who seeks to give his pupils a wider horizon on literature does so at his peril. (See O'Buachalla, 1980: 353)

It is worth reminding ourselves that Pearse was calling in the quoted article for more English Literature on the syllabus, not less, and for a wider, more liberal notion of curriculum. 'There is no freedom in Irish education', he wrote, 'no freedom for the child, no freedom for the teacher, no freedom for the school . . . but a sheer denial of the right of the individual to grow in his own natural way'. Pearse was uncompromising in spelling out the implications: 'The idea of a compulsory programme of education imposed by an external authority on every child in every school in a country is the direct contrary of the root idea involved in education. Yet this is what we have in Ireland'(O'Buachalla, 1980: 353).

Set text and anarchy

Professor Cox is, I believe, of one mind with Pearse in rejecting the idea of 'a list of set texts'. . . not least because it can give rise to the petrification of some time-bound collection of pseudo-canonical texts. Those who took the Leaving Certificate in the 1960s in Ireland may bear this judgement out. We sweated through the prose of Quiller-Couch while our cousins in London were reading the essays of Orwell in their classrooms. Yet one of the alternatives to set-text courses is a sort of benign anarchy, the like of which prevailed in Irish schools after the institution of an open curriculum in the 1920s by Eoin MacNeill, acting no doubt under the influence of Pearse's precepts. By all accounts, this was enjoyed by exceptionally gifted teachers, who had the capacity to choose interesting and challenging texts, and by their brighter students, who had the ability to savour them. But MacNeill did not abolish the hated examination system (even if he stopped the hateful practice of paying teachers by results) with the consequence that most students faced the ultimate nightmare – an open course followed by a set test. The bleakness of such freedom could not long be tolerated and so by June 1940 a new Minister for Education, Éamon de Valera, restored the prescribed books, the Quiller-Couches and so forth.

I think that a case can therefore be made not for a rigidly confined number of set authors or set texts, but for exemplary lists, each of them to be reviewed, say, every three years or so. Of course, Shakespeare should be a core element of such a curriculum, but the study of Shakespeare should also show how Irish interpreters like Yeats and Joyce or West Indians like C.L.R. James read his great texts 'against the grain' of their own experience. Our grandparents who attended performances of *Henry the Fourth: Part One* did not find in its rich language an elitist or imposed code: rather they sensed very rightly how its verbal energies connected with their own still vibrant Hiberno-English ('I met a man and he going to the fair' etc.). Playwrights like Yeats and Synge picked up on these elements in Shakespeare, reworking them in up-market works of art but so also did the railway porter in Limerick station who, in response to Anew McMaster's enquiry through a carriage-window as to whether his team of players had now reached Limerick, instantly responded: 'Why, sir, this is Illyria'.

We, too, have politicians who like at moments of pressure to quote the great texts, though in our case the ultimate source is not Wonderland but Shakespeare. Charles Haughey quoted Othello on his day of departure in lines ('I have done the state some service') which now carry even more vibrations than they did when first he recited them. Mr Jack Lynch loved to quote Polonius ('To thine own self be true. . .') and seemed quite as oblivious to the fact that Polonius in giving the advice was adjudged a meddlesome old buffer as was Joyce's Mr Deasy to the fact that the Iago whom he quoted ('Put but money in thy purse. . .') was the villain of his particular play. Shakespeare can be indeed a weapon of moral exposure, exposing those who quote him as often as those against whom the quotation is intended to be directed.

A range across time and place

Unlike Professor Cox, perhaps, I believe that in order to convey some sense of the slow, magnificent evolution of English literature, we should expect students to know the work of at least one metaphysical poet, one of the Augustans, a Romantic and a Victorian author, as well as a range of modern writing, not just in these islands but in the wider English-speaking world. This would help to reawaken in students what so many today badly lack – a definite sense of chronology, of some writers following, being enabled (and intimidated) by others, of tradition as a perpetual act of negotiation with the past. In that context, contrapuntal readings of, say, *The Tempest* and *The Color Purple*, *Jane Eyre* and *Wide Sargasso Sea*, *Heart of Darkness* and *Season of Migration to the South* would work very well, offering students something more than the sum of each of their parts. And that reminds me just how right Professor Cox was to quote those lines questioning all myopic cults of immediate 'relevance'. Young people are as interested as any of us in a world elsewhere and that is just a homely way of saying what T. S. Eliot more beautifully talked of in his essay on Shakespeare's *Twelfth Night* – 'a recognition, implicit in the expression of every experience, of other kinds of experience which are possible'.

Those who wrote the classic texts of literature in earlier ages did so in the blithe assurance that their control of global discourse would last forever. In constructing that narrative, they offered native peoples everywhere a priceless, if ambiguous, gift: the story of how they had been banished from their own land. Those natives have since learned how to read and reread the texts that ignored or misrepresented them, texts that assumed that they could never intervene. It is vital to retain these, not just for their intrinsic beauty and value, but for the sharpness and confidence with which they render a monocultural world. Otherwise, we shall all be in such a hurry to revise that we shall forget what it was that stood in such need of revising.

The sorry history of Irish-language texts in the island's class-rooms since the 1920s should remind us that not all the imperfections and incompletenesses in a society can be put right by a nation's teachers or chosen texts – and that a culture risks being mummified rather than revitalised in a classroom. Current calls by 'minority' groups for books which answer to their experience with idealised role-models are an understandable response to centuries of repression, but there is a danger that they may lead to a tedious rectitude in texts, such as offended students of the Irish language in the decades after independence. Similarly, the relentless insistence on books which contain characters with whom students might identify is a denial of an elementary function of literature: its delight in encountering other voices and other worlds than our own. To seek to identify fully with a character or text is to fall victim to the same quality of essentialist thinking which caused so much suffering for members of minority groups in the first place. Equally, to conduct head-counts of the number of blacks, northerners, women, Hindus or whatever represented in anthologies or syllabi is to debase debate to levels of quantity rather than quality, and to forget that classic texts need not so much to be discarded as reread and put into vibration with the texts from the newer world.

Strictures and the remarkable soul

I am in full accord with Professor Cox's insistence that language is what people speak rather than a set of old-fashioned rules about split infinitives. (It is one of my proudest boasts that I have never 'corrected' a student essayist who split an infinitive, though honesty compels me to add that I have secretly continued to think far better of the students who steadfastly refuse to do so.) Shakespeare was not the only great writer who lived in ignorance of the semi-colon: Michael Yeats once recalled how a major American scholar asked whether his father would have employed a colon or a semi-colon at a certain line-ending in his great poem 'The Statues'. 'Papa would never have known the difference' chortled his son. The recent publication of W.B. Yeats's Letters gives every struggling student of English some grounds for hope – the poet routinely misspelled such words as feel (feal), night (nigth), and he forever blighted his chances of the Chair of

English at Trinity College Dublin by misspelling the word *professorship* in his letter of application. Yet one has only to read his handling of the slow accretion of clauses in 'Among Schoolchildren' to recognise that he was able to realise all the expressive potentials of the English language.

What Professor Cox says about the need to reconcile language as activity and language as system is useful here, not just as an account of the imaginative compromises which are struck daily in all good classrooms, but also as an account of the inner workings of art. After all, every writer receives her or his language in a certain condition, as a system with a whole deposit of cliches and recommended phrases for the use of learners. The dream of every writer is somehow to produce a personal language so charged with individuality as to leave the given language in a drastically changed state. Mediocre authors tend to surrender too early and too obviously to the received codes of the system. Daring dissidents from those codes run the risk of being labelled, like the Joyce who wrote *Finnegans Wake*, autistic. But between those extremes is a blessed zone in which a true genius strikes a balance. And that balance returns us to the prior challenge of the classroom – the fear that those who know how to feel often have, as yet, no capacity to express themselves and yet, by the time they are old enough to have acquired the expressive capacity, many have forgotten how to feel. Only rare, remarkable souls manage to seize a received language and inflect it with the rhythms of individual feeling.

I would also endorse the argument that Received Pronunciation should not be enforced. Its enforcement has robbed us (almost) of the rich Hiberno-English which so impressed Yeats that he called for its use and sanction in such 'prestigious' activities as church sermons, newspaper editorials and college lectures. But, sadly, people's minds were so colonised that they could under-stand only the imitation of standard English rather than the brilliance of their own prior expressive achievement in Hiberno-English, an act of radical creation rather than mere imitation. Does anyone really believe that the virtual loss of that expressive ensemble has done anything to enhance the expressive powers of Irish individuals?

Oral communication precedes all written forms and should, accordingly, be prioritised. This doesn't always happen. When I

lived with my young family in California in the mid-1980s, I told
the children nightly stories out of my head. At school the teacher
kept a log-book recording their reading, but when asked whether
the 'head-stories' could be entered along with 'book-readings' in
the ledger, responded with a flat refusal. In post-Reagan California,
the attempt to return to the three Rs was being carried so far that
parents carried stickers on their car-fenders which went 'Did You
Read to Your Kid Last Night?' In such a reactionary world, what
was not on the printed page did not count at all – yet the irony
was that when schoolyard fights broke out, children were invariably told by teachers 'Use your words, can't you? Use your words.'
Nonetheless, all expression in class seemed mediated through
acts of writing.

The results of that return to basics are now manifest in the fact
that Junior Year Abroad students at Irish colleges are every bit as
good as their local counterparts at written work: something that
was not always true. On this side of the Atlantic, a generation of
students has emerged with formidable gifts for formulating
abstract ideas in debate, but often with very little notion of how
to turn the presentation of those ideas into clear, paragraphed
essays of discursive prose. Professors are now seriously considering the need for some equivalent to the US courses in the
higher literacy and 'Freshman Composition' . . . even for post-
graduates. People in industry report similar needs for training
and retraining those who write business reports. And newspaper
editors may often be heard lamenting the fact that their most
brilliant investigative journalists often sell a good story short
through inadequate writing skills. This is clearly not a problem
that afflicts only the unintelligent. In fact, it bedevils most people
whose powers of written expression often lag well behind their
capacity for analysis and conceptualisation.

'Practical' English

Having said that much, I would like to add a final observation.
However much we debate the canon or the value of Shakespeare
or the quality of regional dialects or the search for a serviceable
prose style, we should remember that most people in the world
now studying English wish to know it only as a technical or
computer language, an international code in which the efficient

services of the modern world are supplied. Many, perhaps most, who study it are not seeking to expand their expressive freedom so much as pursuing a logical economic advantage. Even in those countries to which English was brought as part of the colonial enterprise, this is true. If today a young Egyptian wishes to work for an international airline, English is the gateway – and an English with no aesthetic dimension. That is a chilling thought, in some ways, as chilling as the story of the young Nigerian who wrote to Chinua Achebe praising his novel *Things Fall Apart* and regretting only that it lacked one vital dimension: '. . . you did not supply any model exam questions at the end of the text'.

However, lest we get too depressed by all this, we should remember that James Joyce made his living while writing his masterpieces by teaching *Berlitz* English to foreign businessmen. It was, indeed, from that experience, he said, that he developed his fascination with the unfinished sentence, the one that starts confidently before petering out into inconclusiveness. Every English teacher who ever stood before a blackboard will recognise that phenomenon, but Joyce showed how even such unpromising moments can be turned to the most creative use. And in that lies a measure of hope for all.

References

O'Buachalla, S. (ed.) (1980) *'A Significant Irish Educationalist' – The Educational Writings of P.H. Pearse*, Dublin: Mercier Press.

Reynolds, H. (1934/1970) *Letters to the New Island*, Cambridge, MA: Harvard University Press.

Part 2

Listening, speaking, reading and spelling

4
Teaching reading comprehension across the curriculum
Elizabeth O'Gorman

In this chapter I will restate the case for a cross-curricular approach towards teaching English language skills. Then I will outline a programme, the Junior Certificate School Programme, in which such an approach is being utilised. The focus will be on the area of reading comprehension, specifically in the area of 'expository' (factual) texts. Finally, I will suggest some practical strategies that can be used in any subject area to enhance the teaching of expository text skills.

The need for a cross curricular approach to teaching reading skills

Good reading comprehension skills and writing ability underpin academic success in most areas of the curriculum. Students who develop the ability to use these skills in dealing with a range of text types are likely to derive greater benefit from their educational experience than are those without such skills. Responsibility for developing these reading and comprehension skills rests mainly with the English teacher but perhaps, in line with a cross-curricular approach to teaching language skills, other subject teachers can both share in the development of these skills and benefit from them.

In schools the majority of texts which students encounter are expository, subject area texts. These texts – in History, Geography, Environmental and Social Studies (ESS), Science and so on – usually differ in structure and content from the narrative type of text which forms the bulk of the English syllabus. Because of the difference in structure between factual and narrative texts, different skills are required to comprehend and produce these texts.

Unfortunately, up to recently, little attention has been given to the direct nurturing of these skills. In the English class the development of reading comprehension skills revolves mainly around novels and short stories; the development of writing skills focuses largely on creative writing. These areas are essential for personal development as well as examination purposes and, as they are time intensive, they leave little opportunity for training students to deal with expository texts. Now that the Junior Certificate English syllabus and examination contain more factual types of text there has been a move towards developing student skills in this area. Research shows that time spent in direct reading instruction in the expository area is rewarded by improvement in both reading and writing skills (O'Gorman, 1995).

In addition to developing skills with expository texts in the English class, students also need help in transferring the skills from the context of the English class to other subject areas. Unfortunately, such transferral is not automatic. Concurrent training in dealing with these text types in both the English class and other classes would help to ensure that the skills have wide application. However, in the non-English class the main focus is on the subject content itself. Consequently, there is little attention given to teaching the skills necessary both to access and to produce factual texts. If it were possible to initiate a school-wide approach to teaching expository text skills, the additional repetition, reinforcement and wide ranging examples would help to establish these essential but often neglected skills.

In primary schools it is usually the same teacher who oversees the development of English skills and subject area skills. Therefore, the opportunity to develop language skills occurs both in the

English class (through stories, for example) and in other content areas through factual texts. Because of this overlap it is feasible for primary teachers to successfully undertake the development of expository text skills. At post primary level, subjects are likely to be taught by subject specialists whose attention is directed mainly to the content aspect of the text. Some subject teachers may opt to develop students' comprehension skills or to improve their writing skills or even improve spelling. In general, however, not only is this perceived as time consuming but also, unless the subject specialist has had specific training in the area, it is thought to be an area best left to the English teacher. On the other hand English teachers are mainly focused on opening 'windows of wonder'. They are offering experiences of other lives for pupils to reflect on, developing creative writing skills, developing the pupils' ability to respond to literature, developing their self expression and all the other aspects of English teaching that go beyond covering the syllabus. As with other subject teachers they too are unlikely to have the time to develop expository text reading skills.

It is interesting to speculate on how far teachers have moved from the position described in Durkin (1979). She found that three per cent of reading comprehension time was spent on direct reading instruction and noted that although teachers gave sufficient information on a skill for students to complete a task, they did not teach reading comprehension skills directly. The assumption would seem to be that reading comprehension skills will gradually be acquired through an osmosis-type effect if students work through an adequate number of practice exercises. The difference between teaching and testing is often minimal in such circumstances. There is clearly no acknowledgement of the notion that practice must be preceded by direct instruction for learning to take place.

When all subject teachers collaborate on a programme of teaching reading skills this important area need not be neglected due to lack of time. The work involved will not only be shared but also be more effective.

**Teaching English within the framework of the
Junior Certificate School Programme – a cross
curricular approach**

Facilitating post-primary teachers to work as a team can be
difficult within the traditional second-level school structure.
First, teachers have to be convinced of the advantage of such
collaboration. Next, appropriate materials – which focus and
guide through similar approaches in the various subject areas –
have to be found. Then the timetable constraints have to be overcome to organise suitable meeting time. The Junior Certificate
School Programme[1] brings together ways of addressing some of
these problems. The programme incorporates the opportunity
to adopt a whole-school approach to teaching basic skills in the
Junior Cycle. Within this programme a team of teachers work
together to adopt a common policy towards teaching potential
early school leavers. This includes the option of a cross-
curricular approach to the teaching of language skills.

In essence the aim of the Junior Certificate School Programme
(JCSP) is to make the experience of school relevant and accessible
to those young people who find it difficult to cope with the
school system and who are potential early school leavers. The
main features of the JCSP are:

• Small teaching teams and regular team meetings
• A reduced number of subjects with a well thought out
  curriculum
• A cross-curricular approach
• Short-term achievable goals
• Active, experiential learning
• Feedback to students with acknowledgement of success
• Attention to social and personal skills as well as academic and
  practical skills
• Feedback to parents
• Links with the primary school

The Junior Certificate School Programme is the outcome of an
initiative that began in 1979 within the CDVEC's Curriculum
Development Unit. Over the years the good ideas and practices

that helped teachers to make school and schoolwork more interesting and relevant for potential early school leavers were distilled to form the basis of the programme. In addition to focusing on social and personal development and basic subject skills, the programme helps to guide and support *at risk* students while they are working towards the Junior Certificate. The JCSP is an intervention into the current Junior Certificate curriculum. It is not an alternative programme. Various Junior Certificate subject syllabi have been scrutinised and the fundamental elements of each isolated. These elements are listed as statements about a student's ability in each subject. The statements are broad and the level is akin to that which is expected during the course of the Junior Certificate. For example, in English one of the statements is as follows:

The student can, at Junior Certificate Level, use written language to express and reflect on experiences.

Each statement is broken down into approximately ten subsections. These serve two purposes. They are indicators of when to award the statement and also are useful guidelines for teachers in setting out a focused course of work towards achieving the statement. These are the guidelines/objectives for the above English statement:

Guidelines

This has been demonstrated by the student's ability to:

1. Write a brief note or paragraph about a personal experience or interest, for example for a diary or journal.

2. Write three paragraphs about a personal experience or interest, for example for a letter to a friend.

3. Give a written account of specified personal likes and dislikes, for example favourite musicians.

4. Write a note or paragraph expressing the experiences of seeing, hearing, touching, tasting.

5. Write a note or paragraph expressing the emotions and experiences of a given situation.

6. Write a note or paragraph expressing a preference or opinion about a given situation.

7. Produce a piece of writing responding to a letter, story, poem, book, film, newspaper or TV programme.

8. Imagine the ending of story, background of a character or event and write it.

9. Re-read, revise and correct own writing.

(from *The Junior Certificate School Programme Handbook*, 1998 edition)

Students' performance on statements and learning objectives are recorded in three stages:

■	❑	❑	Work Begun
■	■	❑	Work in Progress
■	■	■	Work Completed

Teachers, and students themselves, chart their progress by reflecting on such areas as: independence; frequency; sustainability and accuracy.

In addition to the individual subject statements there are a number of cross-curricular statements. Some of the cross curricular statements pertain to social and personal development and include concepts and notions such as working together, working alone, punctuality, attendance and so on. Many cover a wide number of subject areas such as Health and Safety, Project Skills, or Activities – for example Measurement which applies to a number of subjects – Science, Home Economics, Materials Technology Wood, Materials Technology Metal, Geography.

Of particular appeal to teachers interested in the area of expository text skill development is the cross-curricular statement on texts:

The student can at Junior Certificate Level retrieve general and specific information from a variety of texts

Here the centrality of reading skills to most subject areas is acknowledged. As with the sample English statement, this cross-curricular statement is broken down into a series of guidelines. These guidelines itemise basic reading skills, which can be applied to any text and to any subject. Guidelines 4–9 deal specifically with identifying the topic and details of texts. The strategies espoused in the practical strategy section of this article are specifically aimed at enabling students to achieve these objectives.

Guidelines

This has been demonstrated by the student's ability to:

1. Use a contents page, an index and a dictionary.

2. Find specific information in an alphabetical index, for example a glossary.

3. Identify sentences, paragraphs and basic punctuation marks in a continuous piece of text.

4. Find specific information in a timetable, league table, menu, advertisement or other similar text.

5. Find specific information in a piece of text, for example a subject textbook or newspaper.

6. Identify the topic/general gist of a short text – using texts from any subject area.

7. Give the main point of a short text – using texts from any subject area.

8. Find details which support the main point of a short text – using texts from any subject area.

9. Follow correctly step-by-step instructions for a recipe, procedure, experiment or exercise routine.

(from *The Junior Certificate School Programme Handbook*, 1998 edition)

Should the team of teachers choose this statement, then two or more will work together on achieving the objectives. In the ensuing weeks the teachers will discuss informally on which aspects they will focus, share materials and identify common areas of concern. Most importantly the teachers inform the students of the short-term goal they are setting and give frequent feedback to the students on their success in progressing towards that goal. Ideally, the teacher and student together fill in the record of progress at the appropriate level – work begun, work in progress or work completed. This feedback and self-monitoring are essential parts of developing students' awareness of what they are trying to achieve in their learning and also of enhancing their metacognitive skills.

Thus, the discussions at team meetings give teachers the opportunity to share their knowledge and resources and to identify ways to complement and reinforce each other's work. This is likely to transfer into a more focused, meaningful course of work for those students who are potential early leavers. Indeed, it has also been found helpful to adopt such an approach with all students, not just those involved in the JCSP, and all or part of the programme can be used to broaden the range of teaching techniques used with the age group.

Some strategies used in the Junior Certificate School Programme for improving students' expository text skills

Following a short outline of the background methodology, this section sketches three of the main reading strategies relating to the JCSP cross-curricular text comprehension statement. Briefly, these are:

- Focusing on higher versus lower order reading skills; CSSD (see p. 45) and SQ3R (see p. 46)
- The use of the K-W-L grid (see p. 47)
- The use of a graphic organiser (see p. 48)

The precise meaning of these terms is explained later: for now it is enough to know that they represent specific, well-tested strategies used to help students to achieve the objectives marked 4–9 above.

The Junior Certificate School Programme espouses active, experiential learning and so it is seen as important to ensure that students are actively engaged in their learning and are not simply passive recipients of a regurgitated text. In introducing the various reading strategies, dialogue with the students and their active engagement with the text is preferred. One recommendation is to 'always read with a pencil in your hand'. A corollary of this is to 'jot down notes, words, anything when reading'. For weak students this can be difficult but if given a simple grid to fill in, as suggested below, their time spent reading becomes much more productive. The success this engenders motivates further attempts at reading and thus the cycle continues.

There are scores of different techniques that can be used to enhance students' ability to deal with text comprehension. *Reading and Writing in Content Areas* (Vacca and Vacca, 1993) provides one of the most thorough compendiums of such strategies. However, any book on study skills will contain an ample supply of ideas. One I personally have found particularly useful is the *Study Skills for VTOS Students* course book (CDVEC, 1995) which contains descriptions of both study and reading techniques and exercises on these. When deciding on strategies to select it is best to limit the number chosen to avoid confusion.

At what point should these strategies be taught? Many schools now offer first-year and transition-year students a study skills course. Perhaps this course could be offered to all students on a regular basis. There is reason to promote their use in primary as well as secondary school. With continuous repetition and reinforcement of these skills in all subject areas and at all stages of their academic career, students will have a better chance of making the most of their educational experience.

Unfortunately, it is not sufficient simply to give students 'tactics' to use.

For significant change to take place in students' reading comprehension skills or study skills the strategies must be taught *metacognitively*. This term is used to describe awareness of the thinking process involved in using a strategy ('Thinking about what you're thinking about' as my students refer to it). Being metacognitive about their reading and learning helps students to:

- be more aware of the purpose of a strategy
- choose an appropriate strategy for the task in hand
- constantly monitor their use of the strategy
- check its effectiveness
- alter their use of the strategy when appropriate

It is difficult to change long established reading and study habits. Teaching these new habits metacognitively has proved more successful than simply giving students a blueprint of the target strategies. Biggs and Rihn (1984) found in their study with academically 'at risk' students that a significant improvement of grades was achieved through using metacognitive approaches to teaching target study habits. Activities such as self-evaluation and having students discuss their learning strategies with others also proved beneficial. This exploration leads students to realise the need for change. Without this realisation, changes in learning and reading habits are unlikely to take place. In summary, for the teaching of any new reading strategies to be effective, it must be accompanied by an awareness of the purpose of the strategy, discussion of its value and self monitoring of the strategy in use.

Higher versus lower order reading skills

When we read a text we use a sampling technique. Goodman (1976) described this as a 'psycholinguistic guessing game' in which readers reconstruct as best they can a message encoded by a writer. Readers do this by mentally predicting what will come next in the text. Because all readers share a common knowledge of word order, sentence structure, semantic webs and other text features, these predictions are likely to be quite accurate. The readers then test their prediction by sampling the text and, on the basis of this sample, confirm or revise those predictions. Goodman asserts that readers rely more on their semantic and syntactic knowledge (higher order reading skills) than on individual word meanings or letter-sound relationships (lower order reading skills).

In addition to this emphasis on overall meaning and the structure of texts, Goodman postulates that readers need not use all of the textual clues available. He points to the redundancy which exists at all levels of language – letter features, within words, within sentences, within discourses, all of which give excess opportunity to readers to create meaning.

Frequently, when faced with a difficult text students revert to lower level reading skills – they rush to the dictionary to find the meaning of every word, and in the ensuing over concentration on individual words, lose track of the overall meaning and consequently comprehension suffers. Thus, the transferral of higher level reading skills to all subject areas is essential. One method of helping with this transferral is for all teachers to put the acronym 'NEW' (Not Every Word) on the board when beginning a new piece of text. This is to remind students that many words in a text are redundant and it is not essential to know every word in a text to be able to understand it. However, this is not to say that students should skip unknown words but rather that they should adopt strategies for dealing with them.

One of the more difficult tasks for teachers and students is identifying the essential vocabulary of a text. This is particularly difficult in subjects with large quantities of technical vocabulary. A common mistake is to have students go through the text underlining all the difficult words. This tends to reinforce the impression that the text is incomprehensible. Rather, ask students to note only those words that hinder their comprehension. Comparing students' and teachers' lists of difficult words can be an interesting exercise; often there is surprisingly little overlap. In cases where the technical vocabulary of a subject area presents difficulty, a useful method of establishing essential vocabulary is to select the main concepts and then choose only those words necessary to explain those concepts. By focusing on the major concepts of a new text, difficult vocabulary items that do not relate to these concepts can be eliminated.

Another useful technique in this area of difficult vocabulary is to introduce students to the notion of three categories for sorting vocabulary items – *active, passive and throwaway vocabulary*. Knowing that words can be classified like this is one of the most helpful strategies in overcoming the fixation with understanding individual words at the expense of overall understanding. Active vocabulary consists of the words students understand and use – their 'idiolect'. Passive vocabulary consists of the words they need to understand but will not need to use. And finally their 'throwaway' vocabulary consists of those words they meet which do not contribute additional meaning in texts and which will never form part of their idiolect. In order for students to become accustomed to attempting texts which stretch their reading capabilities teachers need to take on the role of an inexperienced reader and 'think aloud' their reading process showing through verbal example how they might disregard certain words and hazard a guess at others.

Once students have decided that they need to know the meaning of a word they then use their *word attack skills*. One such approach is CSSD – **C**ontext, **S**tructure, **S**ound, **D**ictionary. This approach to understanding vocabulary allows students to progress through a structured sequence in order to understand a word.

In relation to this sequence three things are of interest. First, there is a downward progression from the higher order reading skills to the lower order reading skills. Second, the student relies on their own internal resources initially. Third, a dictionary is seen as a last resort rather than as a port of first call. This involves an adjustment to the general exhortation – 'use your dictionary!' – when an unknown word emerges from a text. For students to acquire the skills to tackle unknown words this strategy needs to be used frequently and used across all subject

---

CSSD

CONTEXT Students try to work out the meaning by using the context, by rereading the text or by reading on to see if that clarifies the word. Should this strategy fail to resolve the problem students further consider the context. This time they look at the semantic area and try to work out a possible meaning (e.g. 'So this is all about . . . , so I suppose the word must have something to do with . . . Maybe it means something like . . .').

STRUCTURE Next they look at the structure, the affixes, the words function in the sentence, its similarity to other words, and so forth. (e.g. 'It must be a thing or it must be a doing word, it looks a bit like . . .').

SOUND After this, students check the sound. (By saying a word aloud echoes of similar words are sometimes evoked.)

DICTIONARY Finally, if all this fails, a dictionary could be used.

This sequence can usefully be depicted on a flow chart for the classroom wall.

---

areas. Teachers need to model this process out loud for the students. After several demonstrations of how teachers tackle word meaning, students may be able to internalise the strategy. However, repetition during the year is extremely useful to cement the technique.

In light of the fact that the search for meaning is more important than simple word recognition and that this search can be conducted at different levels of depth, it is wise to encourage students to use a variety of different reading styles depending on the purpose of the text. *Scanning, skimming, light reading and careful reading* could be practised with a variety of textbooks either in the English class or in the subject class. Giving students the tools to approach their reading is very empowering.

One such long-established technique is known as SQ3R: *Survey Question Read Recall Review*. This was originally developed in the 1940s and has been amended to give rise to other similar techniques. Its ongoing popularity is due in part to its use in the SRA kits with which many teachers will be familiar. Undoubtedly some of the new versions of SQ3R are more accessible to students but there is little difference in their intent. The most important aspect is that all teachers should use this technique when dealing with new texts. Being in possession of a set of tools to use when tackling a new text is a great boost for a student's self-confidence. The VTOS handbook (CDVEC, 1995) contains a useful introduction to this technique. Rather than use artificial, specially constructed exercises to practise this technique, it is best to make use of the students' own textbooks. If there is not a suitable text in your subject textbook to practise a technique, look at other subjects' textbooks. Before introducing the target reading/study technique, discuss with the students how they currently read / study and what their strategies are. 'I give up' and 'I ask my friend' are two of the most common responses. Indeed both are legitimate responses to an exceptionally difficult task. If the students themselves come to a decision to add a new or different technique to their repertoire they are more likely to be successful in adopting it in the long term.

Being actively engaged in making sense of a text is one of the essential steps in promoting understanding. One way of doing this is to activate students' prior knowledge. There are several strategies one can use here. One of the easiest to use is known as K-W-L. This stands for What I **K**now; What I **W**ant to Know; What I **L**earned (Ogle, 1986). This strategy has the advantage of being applicable to both narrative and expository texts.

In some ways K-W-L is similar to SQ3R in that it follows similar steps of activating prior knowledge, setting questions to be answered through reading, and reviewing what has been read. In addition it has the refinement of an easily drawn grid to help focus on essential elements of the text. Getting students to draw this grid in their exercise book before tackling a text also helps to make them active participants in the search for understanding.

KWL grid

Topic _____

What I know	What I want to know	What I learned

Initially, it is best to model this strategy on the blackboard for the class and to do so on several occasions. Gradually, withdraw support so that students are able to do it in groups, then in pairs and eventually independently. It will take time before students can use it independently to good effect. First, have a brainstorming session. Give a free rein to the students to tell you all they know about the topic. This helps to activate their schemas – setting up mental structures that will enable the new information to fit more easily into their memories and help retain it. After drawing out their ideas as much as possible, fill in the *what I know* column. Initially do this on the blackboard as a class activity. Next, based on any uncertainties thrown up during the previous session, formulate questions to which you would like to find answers. Write these questions in the *what I want to know* column. (Not all the questions will be answered in the text and this may give rise to further research.) At this point students read the text silently. Because they have some idea what the text is about and because they are focusing on answers to their specific questions, they will be more likely to use higher order reading skills. When they have finished reading, students fill in the *what I learned* column. They include in it the answers to questions they asked and additional information they found. One of the benefits of this technique is that it provides a structured procedure for taking notes on a text and another is the limited space it offers to write in. This can help in preventing wholesale copying of a text and is useful in project work.

Using graphic organisers as support for students' reading

Analysing texts on the basis of their rhetorical structure can be useful. In particular it serves to underline the differences between the text types met in narrative English texts and those in other areas. Texts have been divided into various types. The most frequently used categories are *narrative*, *expository* and *persuasive* texts. Narrative texts refer to novels and short stories. Expository texts refer to factual texts and include the sub-categories of chronological texts; process/ sequence texts; cause & effect texts; compare & contrast texts. The final text type, persuasive texts, refers to those that seek to change opinions. These often fall within the expository category. Further exploration of strategies dealing with cause & effect type texts and compare & contrast texts can be found in *Beyond Basic Reading Skills* (O'Gorman, forthcoming).

Most expository texts can be dissected into their component parts. Usually each part has an identifiable topic. Often these texts have a topic sentence at the beginning of the paragraph that eases identification but, if not, it can be determined by the answer to the question: What is this text about?

There is often a main idea similarly identified by asking the question: What is the most important thing the writer is trying to get me to understand?

To figure out the main points supporting the writer's idea ask the question: What does the writer say about this idea?

To enhance students' ability to identify the topic and details of a text, teachers should model the questioning strategy above with any expository text they encounter. Again, with emphasis on the need for a metacognitive approach, it is useful to initiate a discussion of how the students attack a text and how valuable are the various strategies used by the class.

Using a T-chart is a further development of the 'topic and supporting details' analysis of texts. It is one of a range of graphic organisers that can be used to help students comprehend an expository text. A T-chart is a very visual summary of a text. It focuses on three elements of a text: the topic, main idea and the supporting detail. As with other scaffold or support systems that utilise grids, students are forced either to select a few words carefully or use their own words to fill in the grid. This inbuilt impediment to wholesale copying promotes active engagement with the text. Students might begin their perusal of the text by utilising the SQ3R technique or K-W-L grid. Then students draw the T-Chart diagram into their exercise book. Next they ask the questions which help identify the topic, main idea and supporting details. Following this they fill in the details on the T-chart. This gives them a very simple outline of the text.

If all three of these techniques are used to engage the students in the text, it allows for repeated engagement with the text utilising a different focus each time. Repetition is one of the cornerstones of ensuring information is retained, and finding alternative methods of engaging with the text is essential to avoid boredom. Hence the sequence of SQ3R, K-W-L and a T-chart allows for structured teaching over a period of time.

T-chart

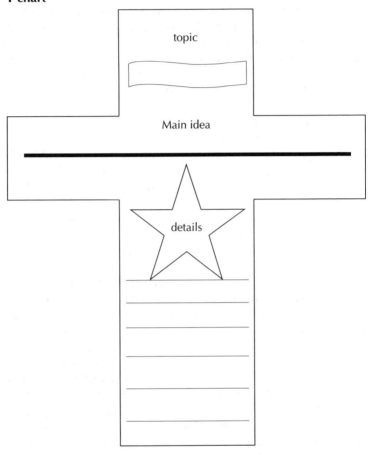

topic

Main idea

details

Sometimes students give up when they encounter difficulty. If you can help them become aware of the fact that everyone has difficulty at times and, more importantly, show them that they have the skills to do something about it, this will empower them. In order to do this they need to use their metacognitive skills and say to themselves: 'I'm having difficulty here. What can I do to solve this?' To remind students of their skills, try putting a flow chart poster on the wall illustrating the sequence of strategies to use. Better still, ask the students to prepare the flow chart; this will actively involve them and be more meaningful than passively seeing your poster. It is not sufficient for students to have been taught the strategies and used these once; they must be used regularly. Have the students draw up the sequence in their exercise books as a reinforcement exercise during the year. Have them draw up the flow chart at different times and in more than one subject notebook to remind them of the universality of the skills. Which skills are used is of less importance than is using them continually.

Conclusion

The strategies outlined in this article were: focusing on higher versus lower order reading skills – CSSD and SQ3R, the use of the K-W-L grid and the use of a graphic organiser. These strategies are not subject specific and can be used by any subject teacher right across the curriculum. These strategies empower students in their reading by giving them a set of tools to which they have access when confronted by a difficult text.

Practice in itself is not sufficient to develop the skills required to handle expository texts. It is important that there is a focused programme of direct instruction in reading skill development. This should incorporate the direct teaching of comprehension skills through teacher modelling and student discussion. One programme that provides the opportunity for a cross-curricular approach to teaching reading skills is the Junior Certificate School Programme. One of this programme's target statements focuses on 'retrieving information from a variety of texts'. Here the teaching of specific reading skills is a goal in itself.

When teachers focus on teaching the content of their subject, whether it is literature or factual information, they give students only that content. When teachers teach reading comprehension skills they give students the key to accessing the content of a multitude of texts – whether in the school setting or beyond.

Notes

1 Contact the Department of Education and Science or the Junior Certificate School Programme support service at the City of Dublin Vocational Education Committee's Curriculum Development Unit for more information on this programme.

References

Biggs J. B. and B. Rihn (1984), 'The effects of intervention on deep and surface approaches to learning.' In: J Kirby (ed.), *Cognitive Strategies and Educational Performance*, New York: Academic Press.

CDVEC (1995) *Study Skills for VTOS Students*, Dublin: City of Dublin Vocational Education Committee.

Durkin (1979) 'What classroom observations reveal about reading comprehension instruction'. *Reading Research Quarterly*, Vol. 14, 481–533.

Goodman, K. (1967) 'Reading: a psycholinguistic guessing game.' *Journal of the Reading Specialist*, Vol. 6: 126–35.

O'Gorman, E. (1995) 'Metacognition and reading', Unpublished thesis. University of Hong Kong

O'Gorman, E. (forthcoming) *Beyond Basic Reading Skills*.

Ogle, D. (1986) 'K-W-L: A teaching model that develops active reading of expository text.' *The Reading Teacher*, Vol. 39: 564–70.

Vacca, R. and J. Vacca (1993) *Content Area Reading*, New York: HarperCollins.

5

Putting spelling in context
Brendan Culligan

My initial task is to examine the deliberate ambiguity in the title of this chapter. It may be interpreted as addressing the position spelling holds in acquiring literacy, or it may be understood to mean that spelling ought not to be taught in isolation by rote learning of lists. Having examined both interpretations, this chapter then looks at the role of the school as an organisation in putting spelling in context, the role of parents, and the roles of the teacher and pupil and how these impinge and depend on each other in providing the positive learning environment that will result in an improvement in children's spelling ability.

Why learn spelling?

If asked why they do spellings, most children will answer that they learn spellings to avoid getting themselves into trouble with teacher or parents! If this is the child's only perception of the function of spelling, then we are failing them. The purpose of spelling is to enable the child to write what he/she wants when he/she wants, that is, to communicate meaningfully. If it is to convey a message, the child's written work must be spelled with some accuracy. If it is not accurate, we may fail to get the meaning, or the teacher in us may home in on the spelling errors and forget what the message was in the first place. In the following lists taken from my research (Culligan, 1996), we may understand what the children who spelled as shown in column A wish to communicate, whereas the same cannot be said of the examples in column B.

A	B
headake	hafllat
anut	nitaes
skar	sriws
wimin	wonsaern

(For the record, the children in group A wished to communicate the same word as those in group B, headake = hafllat, etc). Schonell (1948) stated that 'spelling must be cemented in writing', and I would argue that teaching spelling to the children represented in column B should be put on hold, and attention given to language training. These children do not appear to be ready for purposeful writing and would need a structured language programme whose goal should be teaching children the language they need for reading. Only when the child's language and reading have been sufficiently developed, should he/she be asked to learn spellings.

Many children come to school already able to read and write. Some *catch* spelling in their early school years, but as every teacher knows, there are also those who do not. We are quite fortunate that many children become competent in their written ability, with only minimal direction or supervision. Expecting children to be the architects of their own progress is fine if they have this ability, but we must not treat the strugglers in a similar fashion. These children who struggle with spelling must be *taught* how to spell: they will not pick it up incidentally.

The good and the weak spellers

Before moving on to examine the role of those agents who impinge on the child's education, I wish to contrast some characteristics of the good and the struggling spellers. Good spellers have good linguistic skills. They have no difficulty with the visual perception of word form. They can generalise from the serial probability of letter occurrences and use analogies – for example, by looking intently at words they know that the 'cle' in clever is the same in uncle and clean, and so on. Their visual memory is strong and they do not have difficulty committing words they need to long term memory.

The strugglers are not so fortunate, and if the school (teacher) does not intervene and provide positive and systematic teaching, the child will continue to experience great difficulty and frustration. Spelling is a visual associative process and a hand/eye skill. When the child has a picture of the word in question, the hand takes over and the spelling is written automatically. This automaticity may be demonstrated by writing one's name and address with one's eyes closed.

The most common groups of weak spellers are, first, those with weak visual perception and memory and, second, those who rely on sound to spell. In the latter group, the misspellings become phonetic analogies. Personal observation persuades me that phonetic spelling in many instances may not be due to basic failure in visual perception at all, but to flawed practices that may have been adopted by the children themselves, owing to the lack of an initial strategy. Many come to school already proficient in their knowledge of the alphabet names but find it very perplexing to have to call them by something very different, i.e. sounds. Some find it extremely difficult to understand that sounds of letters, especially vowels, are not always consistent; for example, look/boot.

Some successful teaching strategies

Continued reliance on sound as an approach to learning or teaching spelling is detrimental, and unquestionably will not benefit the under-achiever. The principal reason for confusion among the strugglers is the phoneme/grapheme (letter/sound)

correspondence. If there were a one-to-one equivalence of letters
and sounds, things would be different. One may see that, when we
have 26 letters which give us 44 distinct phonemes, a sounding-out
strategy cannot possibly be consistent. Decoding and reassembling
words are fine in the reading process but sound is a most unreliable basis for spelling. A whole-school approach to the teaching
of spelling is crucial if the struggler is to overcome his/her
difficulties. Cripps and Peters (1990) state that progress in spelling
occurs when teachers' attitudes are consistent and when they are
systematic in their teaching. On the whole, it seems that spellings
are not being taught to those most in need and this practice
needs urgent redress. Peters (1970) aptly summed up the situation
when she stated that 'there is no question that the behaviour of
the teacher determines, more than any other single factor,
whether a child does or does not learn to spell.' It is imperative
that the struggler has a strategy that will enable him/her to move
along successfully at his/her own pace and with words that are
relevant to his/her own written output. We ought not to continue
to assume that teaching to the average ability group, or having
each child – regardless of ability – learn the same list of words is
the formula for a successful approach to the teaching of spelling.
The preferred strategy of this writer for use with most children,
is one that is already in operation in many schools: namely, *Look*
and *Say*, *Picture*, *Cover*, *Write*, *Check* and *Use*.

For those who really struggle, teachers and parents will have
to lower their level of expectations, find out the stage of development they are at, and work at a slower pace until the children
discover that they can do it. The whole school policy must involve
parents. It should focus on the centrality of children's spelling
needs and recognise the huge part that parents have to play in
helping children to improve at spelling. I strongly advocate a
change in the parents' role from one of signing or overseeing
corrections from the weekly test, to that of being actively involved
in helping the child in the learning process. Teachers need to
devote time to explaining to parents how best they may help
their child. Best results will accrue from a team effort where the
child's weaknesses and needs are identified and a programme is
planned accordingly. Such a joint approach can bring about a
substantial improvement with the majority of pupils. A Paired
Spelling Approach could be explained to the parent of the

struggling speller. This may be defined as spending just five minutes working with the child, talking through the words to be learnt, examining the internal structures, looking for words within words or drawing attention to potential blackspots. This undoubtedly would lead to exciting progress and a raising of self-esteem for the child. These five minutes would not necessarily have to be a formal session. More fruitful results would accrue from informal references during the course of the day.

Central importance of teaching strategies

If the teacher has such a crucial role to play, how is it to be utilised to the full? First and foremost, it is not enough for the teacher to be *doing* spelling, instead we must teach spellings to those in need. For some, *doing* spelling means giving the next five words available from their spelling list/book, and then administering the *big test* on Friday. Lists that are irrelevant to children's immediate written requirements are a waste of learning time. Lists which contain words that are neither in the speaking nor reading vocabulary of the child are, according to Schonell (1948), just 'mere verbal lumber'. They will, in all probability, lead to the child's unwillingness to become more responsible for his/her own progress as well as undermining confidence and self-esteem.

Success in the Friday test must not be confused with spelling improvement, and learning lists of words must not be confused with *learning how to spell*, the latter being a skill that needs to be taught. To have weak spellers learning words in isolation for their 'Five-a-night and a test on Friday', is definitely not the best way to enhance children's spelling abilities. Rote memorisation of spelling lists is of doubtful value. Spellings are best put in context (or *cemented in writing*) with words that children need, and these in turn should not be grouped together just because they happen to sound the same. If there is a need for words to be grouped, then as Cripps and Peters (1990) say, it is necessary to group words according to visual structure, thus enabling children to employ associative skills to facilitate learning. Unfortunately in most of the commercial spelling books currently available to Irish children, words are grouped according to how they sound. The concept of teaching spellings through sound is – as we have seen – completely undependable and the segregation of letter-strings from each other, because they do not sound the same, does not make sense. For example, one will never find b*one*, g*one* and m*oney* in the same list.

From early schooling, the role of the teacher should be one of training children to look at words intently. The ideal starting point would be getting the young child to examine his/her own name for other words or common letter strings. For example, in *Stephen* we can find the words *step* and *hen*; M*icha*el and R*icha*rd have much in common; and had my teacher trained me in visual awareness, I would not have had such persistent difficulty with spelling the word cal*enda*r as the letter string causing all the difficulty formed part of my name!

A change of attitude may also be required when correcting spelling. This is an area of great frustration to both teacher and pupil alike. From the teacher's viewpoint there may be the feeling of little or no accomplishment as the same words are written inaccurately time and time again. The pupil on the other hand is very often rewarded (after perhaps a great deal of genuine effort and pleasure on his/her part) with a sea of red pen marks! To remove ourselves from this impasse we need to remember a few salient points.

What the child wants to communicate on paper has to be of prime importance. Reading what he/she is trying to say must always be more important than marking errors. Parents and teachers must do everything possible to ensure that the child's imagination and eagerness to write are not stultified for the sake of spelling perfection. Why not have a dual marking system, one for the story and one for the spelling? Surely, every error does not have to be marked? The teacher will have to decide when to intervene and what kind of intervention is necessary. As Torbe (1977) says, 'a teacher should be helper and guide, not a printer's proof-reader'.

Correcting misspelling

Correcting spelling ought to be meaningful and informative and most importantly it should be done in the presence of the child. What the child does not need is the all too common solution to the error – 'Write it out six times to-night'. This wearisome practice is, arguably, a complete waste of time as it does nothing for the child apart from increasing boredom levels. These 'corrections' may also be viewed as punishment and how often have we seen them to be nothing more than a copying exercise? Children copying words do not think about what they are writing or how to write the words; all they are doing is using eye-hand coordination. This has very little to do with improving visual imagery and memory? Depending on how the child writes these words, he/she may be further exposed to poor spelling. For example, if the child decides it is quicker to write them vertically the error may be compounded, and more than likely this child will not bother to check to see if it is correct.

What is needed with the strugglers' writing is a selective marking system which will mean picking out three or four commonly used words that the child is having difficulty with, and working on those. Torbe (1977) also comments that the teacher's job is not to correct mistakes the pupil has already made, but to help him/her not to make that mistake next time. If a child writes *agen* for *again*, instead of marking it wrong we should mark the *good parts* and praise the very good effort he/she has made (after all, it is 60 per cent correct!). If he/she is not in a position to cross-reference or check the work, talk him/her through what the *bad-spots* are. 'You have a very good picture of the word, but this wrong part or *bad spot* needs to be written like this.' What this child needs to practise is the *ain* letter string as it appears in rain, pain, faint, against, etc. Children's attitudes to spelling change for the better when teachers move away from the *all or nothing* standpoint to one of accentuating the positive aspects of their attempts. For the child it is much more positive to be told that the attempt is almost right.

Contribution of handwriting style to spelling

These final comments on the teacher's role in putting spelling in context for children relate to handwriting style. According to Cripps and Cox (1989), good handwriting and good spelling go together and it would seem logical and more economical to teach them together. If teachers and parents accept this, then the next issue to be considered must be the type of writing instruction/ style to which children need to be exposed; should the children use manuscript (print), or should they use cursive (joined) writing?

While whole-school policies on cursive (joined) writing do exist, the contentious issue among teachers is when it should be introduced. Quite often in their time in Infant classes, children are asked to take a crayon/marker or paintbrush for a walk. This continuous movement across their paper is a natural hand-eye motor-movement, involving many of the actions that are needed in actual letter formation. Printing letters is the opposite of this, but in most of our primary schools the practice is to begin with print and then change over to cursive at a later stage. Within our education system, it is the norm that children learn a style of writing and then later on in their school life unlearn it, in order to acquire a different style. This seems to be questionable time management and practice given that so many of the strugglers tend to reverse and transpose letters. If, as Brown (1990) states, the aim of any aid to handwriting should be to allow maximum use of kinaesthetic memory for words and letter strings, with minimal visual control, there seems little point in teaching children to print. Creating a *running hand* cannot be done by printing. Serious consideration ought to be given to the introduction of such a style as early as possible in the child's school life, that is, when the child has achieved fine motor control. To argue that a cursive style is more difficult for children to both use and read is to underestimate children's ability. If we compare our writing system to that of other European countries we can see what children may achieve when they are exposed to cursive writing from early schooling. The difference is not that French, Dutch or Danish children possess superior motor skills to Irish children, but rather it is to be found in teachers' attitudes and expectations.

Spelling is an important subskill of effective communication. It has to be taught in a systematic and consistent manner to those who do not catch it. Schools that implement a spelling policy which identifies and diagnoses the needs of the child, and then plans a programme which teaches children how to learn, will see an improvement in spelling ability. Trying to improve children's spelling is hard work, but it can be done.

References

Brown, N. (1990) 'Children with spelling and writing difficulties.' In: Pumfrey, P. and C.D. Elliott (eds), *Children's Difficulties in Reading, Spelling and Writing*, Basingstoke, Hants: Falmer Press.

Cripps, C. and R. Cox (1989) *Joining the ABC*, Cambridge: Learning Development Aids.

Cripps, C. and M. Peters (1990) *Catchwords*, London: Harcourt, Brace Jovanovich.

Culligan, B. (1996) 'An Investigation of spelling achievement in the Greater Dublin Area.' *LEARN*, Vol.18. Also in *Education Today*, Autumn/Winter, 1996. Dublin: I.N.T.O.

Culligan, B. (1997) *Improving Children's Spelling*, Dublin: B. Culligan.

Peters, M. L. (1970) *Success in Spelling*, Cambridge: Institute of Education.

Schonell, F.J. (1948) *Backwardness in Basic Subjects* (4th edn), Edinburgh: Oliver & Boyd.

Torbe, M. (1977) *Teaching Spelling*, London: Ward Lock Educational.

6

Listen, Speak and Learn
Mary Howard

In his master classes Augusto Boal frequently says: 'Before all else we see and listen, then we understand.'[1] In the highly educative system of Boal's Theatre of the Oppressed there is a simple exercise which, at its beginning, does not use words at all (Boal, 1992, 1995). It is, if you like, a problem-solving exercise where a series of three group images is made by members of the group in their investigation into their concerns, issues, oppressions:

(*a*) The Image of Reality – the situation as it is

(*b*) The Ideal Image – the situation as I would like it to be, and

(*c*) The Image of Possible Transition – what must happen to get from (*a*) to (*b*).

It is a good starting point to have an ideal image in mind when we begin to think about our pupils and their use of oral language – particularly at a time when we are embarking on a new phase of education, with new curricula on the way, including a move to introduce an oral dimension in the assessment of

English for the Junior Certificate at least. This is a cause for celebration in a country which prides itself on its oral tradition and skill but which, unlike Italy, for example, has not so far honoured this pride in tradition sufficiently in the formal school curriculum.

How does this announcement affect us in our English-speaking primary schools where, it is presumed, language development and oral English have priority every day? I suggest that just having the subject (for want of a better word) talked about is an advantage; it brings it a little bit more under the spotlight and provides us with a welcome opportunity to examine where we stand with regard to the place of oral English in the classroom. Boal, a man of the theatre whose work in education is now known worldwide, often intersperses his workshops with the phrase: 'Always keep in mind the ideal image', that is, keep in mind where you are going, what you ideally wish would happen.

Defining the ideal

So, what is the ideal for Primary School teachers regarding language? Our aim is that all our children will use language fluently and freely and express their ideas clearly, with some degree of authority and even style. This, of course, implies that our children will have opportunities to learn and practise this skill. It implies also that they will be listened to: 'Otherwise', as Richard, a remarkable seven-year-old in my class with severe visual impairment, said to me recently, 'otherwise what's the point? There is no point in speaking, teacher, if nobody is listening.' Richard's insight alerts us to the fact that people are significant: each is a unique existence, to be respected and appreciated as such. But he also reminds us that as human beings we can only live out and assert this unique life in relation with others: to become fully ourselves, to grow into maturity as persons we must enter into relationships which are free, spontaneous and reciprocal.

Laying aside for a moment thoughts of any sort of formal or academic purpose to language, we need to remember that oral language is the basic tool with which human beings make friends, earn their living and become participating members of the community. It is largely through speech that children assimilate the thoughts, opinions, ideas, emotions, humour, wisdom, viewpoints, moral and, indeed, spiritual values of those around them. It is through perceptive listening and effective use of the spoken word that we try to move towards breaking down social, professional and racial barriers. Indeed, we are made painfully aware of the primacy of the spoken word in Ireland today; if Northern Ireland's problems are ever to be solved, it will largely be by talking, talking, talking. It must follow then that the spoken word – in this case Oral English – is one of the most important of all educational activities. But is it given the attention that it deserves in our curriculum?

Speaking and listening: the reality

We may, indeed, all agree on an ideal, that is, something close to what was suggested above. But teachers also know the reality. Many teachers may find the subject – the teaching of listening and speaking skills – difficult. Given the constraints and daily challenges of the classroom, the ideal may seem unattainable. Certainly it often seems to me that the school day militates against sustained listening and speaking in the classroom. Teachers, through no fault of our own, seem under constant pressure to 'cover the curriculum' while keeping classes which are too large busy or quietly occupied (usually by writing exercises). While doing this, they must also find some time to hear each child read, to give an essential few minutes one-to-one to a weak Mathematics student, or to deal with a row in the yard.

Yet if, as often argued, 'every lesson is a language lesson', then oral language work is all the time being carried on in the classroom. This claim is misleading because every lesson is not a language lesson. Curriculum and time imperatives on the teacher to get the 'main teaching points' of the lesson covered have to take precedence. As a result, during these lessons, oral expression remains peripheral though valuable, incidental rather than central, in affording opportunities for listening and speaking.

It is generally accepted that children learn to talk in four ways: by listening to others, by imitating what they hear, by having frequent opportunities to express themselves, and by encouragement and positive correction. Teachers, at every level in school, should be alert to the value and importance of specific lessons for the purpose of listening, speaking and learning – if you do the first two, the third element of the sequence will follow. Joyce recorded his own thinking process in this regard as a young boy in his first year in Clongowes when he noted that by 'thinking of things you could understand them' (Joyce, 1977: 65). What I am advocating is the language lesson that is not a Nature lesson, or a Religion lesson or whatever but one whose specific aims and objectives are centred on listening to children using language, and which gives the subject the focus and, indeed, the status it deserves.

The ideal needs to be made manageable. It becomes so when it is expressed in a couple of specific, realistic, achievable objectives. When I worked for a term on a Youth Enterprises Project in the north inner city, my objectives were often very simple. For example, in one class, Josephine, Peter and Elaine would each give at least three sentences on whatever was the theme of the lesson. Naturally they were not aware of my lesson plans! But it was a manageable goal for teenagers whose concentration span I timed to be about thirty seconds on any subject, but whose intelligence was sharp as a blade. It is important for a teacher to be delighted with this much, and not to be discouraged. It is perfectly acceptable for learners who are linguistically disadvantaged or shy to say exactly the same as the speaker before them and the teacher must resist the temptation to press them too soon for more. This is probably how they are learning and after a few lessons they will move on.

Listening to children

Contributors to this volume stress that success for young people in the future depends on their ability to read, understand and then write. Before any of these abilities can thrive they must be able to handle the spoken word with proficiency, to clothe their thoughts in appropriate and varied language and to express them with a degree of fluency and confidence. We must listen to children using words. Do they understand what they mean? What kind of word patterns do they have? Do they understand the patterns of how language is put together? We can only know the answers to these questions if we listen to children speaking. So when I chose 'Listen, Speak and Learn' as the title of this chapter I meant it as a truly two-way operation – both pupil and teacher listen, speak and learn. We can only assess children's language needs when we hear them speak and we can only encourage their language development by encouraging them to be good and selective listeners.

I want now to ask two questions. First, can even very young children be self-conscious, shy, and slow to express their opinions? I think so. After the first two Reception years in school where everything is usually wonderful, many children begin to see their ability in language in the same way as they see their ability at other school activities – relative to other children. If children have difficulty in oral expression they begin, however vaguely, to perceive this difficulty. I believe that even as early as around second class, they can begin to withdraw, to say less, because it seems all just too difficult. The other question concerns children who are outgoing, even opinionated. Can such children become inhibited in expressing themselves? In other words, can the world begin to crush them when they find themselves unable to keep up with others more verbally skilled? Yes, sometimes.

Learning to communicate

It is worthwhile to take a closer look for a moment at the oral communication process itself. What is actually going on? Good communication can resemble a piece of poetry, or a delicately balanced game of Ping-Pong. Certainly it is a two-way operation: someone encodes a message in spoken language, someone else decodes that message, makes meaning out of it and, generally, encodes another message back. Depending on context and subject-matter, this 'game' develops its interest, stimulation, colour and texture from the quality of language used, the enthusiasm of the speakers and the relevance of the material being discussed. In a good Oral Communication lesson – Listen, Speak and Learn – we aim for a similar process: there must exist an interdependency of listener and speaker – a continuous interchange of roles.

At a workshop given by Boal in London in 1992, I was struck by his remarks – which I noted at the time – on our interdependency as human beings. 'We sense a sound because we hear silence; we smell a flower because we know the smell of bad odours; I am white because there are black people; I am human because you exist; I have my own identity, of course, but because of you.' In the context of our task as nurturers of the spoken word I would like to add that my opinion is valuable because you affirm it, but I will learn only to express that opinion in an atmosphere where there is trust and respect – a safe sort of freedom. The freedom to try out my ideas, ideas I may not yet be very sure of, ideas that may seem unimportant and indeed pretty daft to a fully-fledged man or woman of the world. Yet, these may very well be children's first tentative steps into the area of semi-public utterance, into negotiating the Bigger Issues, *into an area of expression and learning whose success will determine their whole future*. To gain strength and confidence, children must feel that they have the right and the space to *make mistakes*. For the teacher concerned with Oral Communication, then, school must be a place where children are not afraid to make mistakes.

Sharing the space

There is no doubt that a greater emphasis on oracy in the classroom may very well demand quite a change-round for some of us. We will always be 'the teacher' and indeed the child wants that too – but we can shift the distance between us, we can give the child more autonomy, we can share the space. To do this we must opt for comfortable, manageable ground-rules that can work for everybody, while still creating an atmosphere where during this lesson *there is no right or wrong answer but where every contribution is valued and seen to be valued*. When given that chance in class I believe, and I have observed, that young children do generally develop, some even blossom, however slowly, and their confidence and oral skills do improve. In addition, in a well-balanced class, pupils also learn the all-important skill of courteous listening which is an essential element in developing their own language ability in class and in the wider world outside. Recent emphases in education have been so much on active participation (and in general, rightly so) that we have, perhaps, lost sight of a child's need for quiet time, the need sometimes to be serene and to listen. We need to remember that passivity and activity are polarities belonging to the same world. In addition, in our noisy world, children need and deserve to experience the value of silence, to wait while another child thinks of her reply, to experience the courage and confidence that it takes to hold a silence, albeit a short one when one is young. There are times to move, times to be quiet, to sit and listen, to take turns.

The stuff of life

Sometimes the learning that takes place in school can appear rather artificial. I am thinking of the workbook, the imagined situation, 'the text'. Poetry, story and drama are, however, the stuff of life and not merely diversions from it. Without doubt it is imperative that we enter into the magical world of *good quality* stories in our work. Moreover, it is essential that children hear poetry every day if possible, since it taps into their natural feel for rhythm and words. As Kevin Williams points out in chapter 1, young people show a capacity to respond to the rhythm and mood of poetry even where the language is complex and allusive. But we must listen and observe and make sure that children *can and do transfer whatever linguistic skills they learn in these contexts to their own lives*. In drama the opportunities are almost endless. Here, the 'I' of now can dip into the 'I' of the past and negotiate the possible 'I' of the future. If children can practise a role in the aesthetic space of the classroom, then maybe they can use that experience elsewhere. The teacher can also turn a story into a piece of drama. Again one can opt for simplicity – very short scenes and plenty of turn-taking. Children in pairs can in turn play the same short encounter (when Goldilocks first meets one of the Bears, when Naoise first meets Deirdre). Again, what does it matter if each Goldilocks and each bear says the same thing? It marks a start, they will soon get braver and anyway there is always going to be the more adventurous one who will try new ground and pave the way for others. Within the structured freedom which needs to exist around these sort of activities, we are of course obliged promptly to discourage a child who may try to subvert the activity. However, it is consistently observed that when the context derives from children's own concerns they normally respond positively to it. This is also true of adults!

The need for intervention

It is hard to 'catch up' in school, and when children come in who are severely disadvantaged linguistically, it can seem impossible to catch up. But we know we do not have the right to give up. This challenge is part of what it is to teach. To learn how to negotiate the nooks and crannies of higher levels of language – implicit meaning, hidden meaning, inference – sub-text, if you like – the developing mind and linguistic potential need to be given plenty of opportunity to practise oral language skills. Such potential can thrive much more readily, indeed may be able to thrive only when given the space and chance to practise. We are all in agreement on the importance of early intervention, and we agree also that the ideal is intervention at home as well as in the school. Intervention at home can mean switching off the television – the child in my class with the most severe language difficulty has five sets in his home.

Intervention in the classroom often means that we have to prompt verbally to the point of giving children simple words which we may have assumed they knew. This can even be necessary in teaching adults as I have discovered in work in management training. The student was always grateful, inevitably remarking that he or she wished there had been more time for oral language at school. The important factor here, of course, remains that, having been given the words, students at any age must be given the opportunity to use them, to possess them, to make them their own.

Let the body speak too

Though our main concern here is oral language it is vital to remember and make good use of the happy fact that not all communication is verbal, and that one sort of communication can indeed help another. Drama and movement encourage the expressivity of the body as an emitter and receiver of messages and they allow for the use of the body to be part of a dialogue, an extroversion. These activities start from the principle that the human being is a unity, an indivisible whole whose emotions and sensations are all indissolubly interwoven. Observe children who move spontaneously according to the sense or sound of what they are reading, saying or hearing. Augusto Boal's Games, Exercises and Image work (which can be used with students of all ages) emphasises the importance of the body as a means of expression and makes the activities easily accessible (Boal, 1992, 1995). An additional welcome outcome of using some of this work is that it does not privilege the verbally skilled. That said, all the exercises *can* be extended into language development work. Moreover, Boal's beautiful series of exercises for the senses encourage us to *feel* what we touch, to *listen* to what we hear, to *see* what we look at, to stir the memory of the senses. Here knowledge is acquired via the senses as well as the mind.

The human body has its own role in learning. When the senses are stimulated, when the body expresses, voice and language often follow. This results from the acquisition of a new kind of freedom based on mastery of another way of expressing oneself. More in-service training in meaningful Drama-in-Education for all teachers is vital as time and some training are necessary to learn to do this kind of work. In this area, even some basic training can have significant results. Such training must take cognisance of the constraints of classroom life, yet be able to find all the potential there as well, and tap into the good will and natural talent of so many teachers.

Words and language thrive in an atmosphere that is open and has an aesthetic dimension to its structure. There is joy to be found in observing the excitement of the discovery of the spoken word, in being an essential partner in the ebb and flow of a linguistic collaboration that can only enrich that unique relationship between pupil and teacher and carry it perhaps beyond what words can ultimately articulate. To paraphrase our own master of words, Brian Friel, this kind of learning is perhaps 'beyond [our] kind of scrutiny' (Friel, 1984: 309–10). In such an atmosphere real education is taking place, horizons beckon which might otherwise have appeared out of reach. This is every child's right.

Note

1 The direct quotations from Boal are taken from workshops that I attended.

References

Boal, A. (1992) *Games for Actors and Non-Actors*, translated by A. Jackson, London: Routledge.

Boal, A. (1995) *The Rainbow of Desire*, translated by A. Jackson, London: Routledge.

Friel, B. (1984), *Selected Plays,* London: Faber & Faber.

Joyce, J. (1977) *A Portrait of the Artist as a Young Man*, London: Granada.

7
Children's leisure reading
Valerie Coghlan

For many children, childhood is far from being the best time of their lives, or, if it is, this reflects sadly on the rest of their lives. Child abuse, drugs, pregnancy in teenage and even pre-teen girls, homelessness – these are only a few of the horrific situations which young people encounter, it seems all too frequently, either directly or among their peer group.

Anyone who believes in the value of books and reading in the lives of human beings, and in particular in the young, must feel a sense of futility when picking up a newspaper to read yet again about some awful incident involving a child victim. What use are books to children in these situations which we now hear about every day, and which those who teach encounter in classrooms? This question raises others. Does fiction published in Ireland reflect the lives of Irish young people? Or indeed should it?

Early writing for children in Ireland

Looking at books published in the Republic of Ireland, it is interesting to note that a high proportion are what might be classified as 'historical fiction'. These are followed by fantasy, mostly in the 'Celtic fantasy' mode, drawing richly on myths and legends and to some extent on historical incidents. However, books which reflect the lives of contemporary young Irish people are in the minority, and it is not unfair to say that a proportion of these could be described as ephemeral in their appeal. There are a number of reasons why this is so.

Declan Kiberd has suggested that there is a link between colonisation and writing for children, and in *Inventing Ireland* he suggests that in nineteenth-century Ireland 'to write a book-length celebration of an Irish childhood was to flirt dangerously with the stereotype of the childlike Hibernian peasant' (Kiberd, 1996: 105). In *The Big Guide to Irish Children's Books* (Coghlan and Keenan, 1996), Celia Keenan stresses 'the particular importance' of the historical novel 'in colonial and post-colonial cultures'. She states that there is a 'very high interest in history in the wider Irish culture'. There is also the demand of the market – historical fiction sells well into schools.

Jeremy Addis, also writing in *The Big Guide to Irish Children's Books* (Coghlan and Keenan, 1996), is of the opinion that the pervasive, largely conservative moral and cultural climate of the early years of Irish independence had something to do with the paucity of publishing for children during much of this century – apart that is, from school books and the Irish language publications of An Gúm. He remarks:

> It is all the more remarkable then that the current indigenous Irish publishing (including that in the Irish language) is – no doubt partly in reaction against such attitudes – strong in new ideas, new moralities, social realism and experiment. (1996: 15)

Addis is here referring to all publishing in Ireland, and not just publishing for children, for whether publishing for younger readers is yet notable for its strength in terms of 'new ideas, new moralities, social realism and experiment' is a very debatable point.

Where maturity *is* evident in Irish writing and publishing for young people is in historical fiction. Now, periods and incidents which until very recently were far too contentious to form a background for a children's book, have provided a setting and informed the plot of books such as Gerard Whelan's *The Guns of Easter*, set during the 1916 Rising, Mark O'Sullivan's *Melody for Norah* and Aubrey Flegg's *Katie's War*, both of which are set in the Civil War period.

Irish publishing in any quantity for children has not had a long history, and in particular publishing in what might be termed a realistic mode has been even shorter. Authors such as Patricia Lynch and Eilis Dillon, who wrote and published (mainly in the UK and US) in middle years of this century, while writing about contemporary children, introduced an element of fantasy in the case of Lynch, and in the case of Dillon, exciting adventures, as was the fashion in children's books of the period. Dillon's protagonists tend to come from relatively humble rural Irish backgrounds, and that is something with which many children of the time could identify. However, they frequently experienced a level of freedom which, even at a time when parents worried less about their children's whereabouts, was often unconvincing, and most certainly they experience a freedom from the usual emotional and physical preoccupations of adolescence.

The output of the writers published in Ireland at this time also reflected a largely idealised, romantic or heroic outlook. In the early 1970s the Institute of Race Relations in London published a list of books for the children of Irish immigrants to Britain. None of the fiction on this related in any realistic sense to the lives of Irish children of the time – mainly because such fiction was not available. Irish young people were reading British and American novels. Undoubtedly, some of these would have been what Sheila Egoff described as 'the problem novel' (Egoff, Stubbs and Ashley, 1980). Comparing the realistic novel with the problem novel, Egoff comments:

> But while the realistic novel may have conflict at its heart, this is integral to plot and characterisation, its resolution has wide applications, and it grows out of the personal vision of the writer. In problem novels the conflict stems from the writer's social conscience: it is specific rather than universal, and narrow in its significance rather than far-reaching. (1980: x)

The realistic teenage novel

While the realistic novel may be appropriate to a wider age-range, 'the problem novel' tends to be aimed at teenagers or pre-teenagers who read teen fiction. What then of the lives of young people in Ireland in the 1990s in fiction?

Margrit Cruickshank's *Circling the Triangle*, published in 1991, was hailed by a number of commentators as Ireland's first realistic teenage novel. It is narrated by Stephen, a middle-class, south Dublin sixteen-year-old who experiences many of the turmoils of adolescence: trouble at home, trouble in school, unrequited love, lack of appreciation of his music. The novel follows Stephen through a particularly challenging period in his life, and concludes by offering three alternative endings, expressing the lack of certainty experienced by Stephen and many like him.

In general, in Irish realistic fiction it is young males rather than females who are the greater victims of self-doubt. Presumably this is, to some extent at least, based on the many newspaper articles which have appeared in the past few years in which the role of young men is portrayed in a negative, almost despairing light. It is inevitable that this will find an echo in fiction, but it must pose difficulties for authors who also want to offer their readers some reason for optimism.

Cruickshank's next book, *The Door*, also has a teenage male protagonist, Hugh. Much more upbeat in tone and in ending, it shows Hugh and a group of his contemporaries getting involved in a school newspaper, *The Door*, as a means of publicising the sexual harassment of female pupils by a male teacher. Hugh's attachment to his classmate Rachel, who is the editor of *The Door*, develops throughout the narrative, and at the conclusion it may be surmised that it is largely due to Rachel, a strong young woman, that Hugh emerges as a more positive individual.

Jane Mitchell has also tackled the theme of young male alienation in *When Stars Stop Spinning*. As a result of a drunken joyriding escapade in a stolen car, Tony ends up in a coma in an orthopaedic hospital. His rehabilitation and growing attachment to Stephen, another patient, who is dying from a wasting disease, are central to the novel, and it is a brave attempt to show that physical handicap does not exclude young people from many of the usual preoccupations of teenage life.

Music is the common bond between Tony and Stephen, and a desire to make music is also the main concern of Joey in Martina Murphy's *Livewire*. Joey is handsome, bright and talented and about to fail every subject in his Leaving Certificate – not through lack of ability, but deliberately in protest at his father who wants Joey to become an accountant like himself, rather than play in a band and write music. Written *à la* Roddy Doyle, *Livewire* is pacey and peppered with the expletives, which form part of the vocabulary of many people of Joey's age.

The divide between urban and rural communities in Ireland is exemplified in publishing for young people. Almost all books which attempt to reflect the lives of modern young people have urban, or, even more typically, suburban settings, Dublin, and to a lesser extent, Cork, providing the main focus.

Mark O'Sullivan's *White Lies* is one of the few books for young adults set outside a city. A sense of community is often one of the attributes of small-town life, and this is very evident in *White Lies*, as is a strong sense of family. Told in the first person by Nance and her on-off boyfriend OD in alternate chapters, it also contains a cast of adult characters who are significant to the plot. Nance, clever, 17, middle class, is of mixed race and knows that she was adopted as a baby by her parents, Tom and May, who are white. Much of the book is centred on Nance's quest to find her birth mother. She is eventually successful, but not in the way she anticipated, and the book concludes with her realisation that she (and OD) must remake their worlds for themselves.

The sense of family displayed in many books is not confined to parents. Grandparents or other elderly characters frequently have significant roles. In Frank Murphy's *Lockie and Dadge*, Dadge – who rescues runaway Lockie from his unsatisfactory foster home – is not young, and neither is Mammy Tallon nor Pasha with whom Lockie eventually finds a home. In *The Summer of Lily and Esmé* John Quinn has created two remarkable old ladies in Lily and Esmé. Marilyn Taylor shows that older women, in the form of the two grannies, in her trilogy can have very different viewpoints. Hannah's granny in *Hannah or Pink Balloons* by Mary Beckett forms one corner of the tense, triangular relationship that develops between Hannah, who is on the verge of adolescence, her mother, and her granny. The imperfections of older people are openly acknowledged, and many authors have tried to show young readers that being older does not mean being perfect. Rose Doyle in *Goodbye Summer, Goodbye* and Creina Mansfield with *Cherokee*, both show that older people have often sown wild oats in their younger days, and in doing so both authors have created two very memorable older characters.

It is a sign of changing social mores in Ireland, where the family enjoys a highly privileged place in the Constitution, that family groupings in fiction are no longer always in the traditional two parents and child or children mould. Marita Conlon-McKenna in *No Goodbye* explores the reactions of four children aged from six to 14 when their mother walks out of the family home without warning. Told from the alternating perspective of each child, *No Goodbye* makes a brave effort to explain how adult relationships can come to grief.

The plot of *Sisters . . . No Way!* by Siobhan Parkinson hinges on the impending marriage of Cindy's widowed father, Richard, and Aisling's divorced mother, Margaret. *Sisters . . . No Way!*, is written in diary form by Cindy age 15 and Aisling, a year older. It is a play on the Cinderella story, but instead of a glass slipper we have one of Cindy's Doc Martens. The pregnancy resulting from the affair between Richard and Margaret – forcing their ensuing marriage – is typical of a number of novels in which it is the older generation and not the younger, that provides an unexpected fecundity.

The attitudes of authors and publishers to sex in Irish published novels for young adults are ambiguous. Authors writing about teenage emotions are hesitant when it comes to any physical description. Reasons given for this vary from concern about possible controversy, to an embarrassment about writing sex scenes, particularly when the authors concerned know a number of people who may read the book. John Fahy (1996: 52) remarks that Irish fiction does not necessarily need a Judy O'Blume. But there is validity in his point which is that in a country where a number of teenage pregnancies which have had tragic outcomes have received sensational publicity, books are required which deal in a sensitive and non-judgmental way with teenage sex and its possible consequences. Gretta Mulrooney's *Crossing the Line* is compared to Blume's *Forever* in the blurb: 'Not since *Forever* has a teenage novel explored first love and sexuality so openly and honestly'. While it does indeed explore first love and while this is eventually consummated, any reader expecting the explicitness of *Forever* will be sadly disappointed.

Sex and its possible outcome and other controversial matters such as drugs also occur in Irish fiction, but frequently involving secondary rather than primary characters. *When Love Comes To Town* by Tom Lennon is franker, and it is very much a young adult novel in its perspective on teenage Dublin life. Neil is almost 18 and about to leave school. He is gay and his own acceptance of this, and his efforts to make his family and friends understand, form the core of the novel. The setting, and the easily identifiable school attended by Neil, were part of the reason for its publication as an adult book in 1993, but it is now likely that it would be marketed as a book for older young adults.

Conclusion

Peter Hollindale, commenting on 'the adolescent novel of ideas' during the past 25 years, articulates well a dilemma that may be particularly appropriate to consider at this point. He notes the difficulty of even discussing a novel form which at one extreme is a simple 'children's book' (with added sex, violence and family collapse) while at the other is also asking questions about *Homo sapiens* which most adult readers are too frightened or too stuck in their ways to face. Seen from this perspective, the challenge of providing suitable teenage leisure reading material is clearly a formidable one.

It may be that Irish writers and publishers who see a market for books about contemporary issues will create an opportunistic and issue-driven fiction, but this is likely to be tempered by strong concern for their readers and, to some extent, for the more conservative elements of the market. Also, concerns which are experienced in Ireland as elsewhere, about the difficulties of marketing young adult fiction, may create a reduction in output which might have the effect of creating overall higher standards in the content of what is published. So far, Irish publishing for young people has at times tended to a display a 'never mind the quality, feel the width' attitude, which is understandable in a market which is comparatively new and therefore requiring some degree of trial and error.

I am not suggesting Irish publishers should look at potentially controversial issues as topics for their fiction list – if that happens it will result as Egoff suggests in 'novels which are narrow in significance rather than far-reaching' (Egoff, Stubbs and Ashley, 1996). Not all children want to read about 'real life'. The popularity of fantasy demonstrates this. Children who live in difficult circumstances do not necessarily want to read about others who also have difficulties in their lives. Fortunately, many children have a childhood relatively free from trauma of the kinds mentioned, and more fiction which reflects this is also needed.

Referring to the 1997 Carnegie Medal short list, Geraldine Brennan in *The Times Educational Supplement* described it as 'the year of the troubled child'. One can see what she means with books on the short list like Anne Fine's *The Tulip Touch* which was sparked off by the Jamie Bulger case, and *Junk* by Melvin Burgess, the eventual winner, which pulls no punches about heroin addiction. Both of these books are provocative and make disturbing reading. They pose questions at very fundamental levels about the sort of society which modern Britain is offering to young people – and the sort of society in which young Irish people too are growing to maturity.

It is important that choice in reading material is available. Young people read for a variety of reasons among them to help make sense of their lives, and to read about other people like themselves. I am not sure that many Irish novels reflect the lives of the young people who read them – or indeed, of the young people who do not read them. I *am* sure that books should be available which in a responsible way, without preaching or condescending, may help those who read them – even in a very small way.

References

Addis, J. (1996) 'Publishing for children in Ireland.' In: Coghlan, V. and
    C. Keenan (1996) *The Big Guide to Irish Children's Books,* Dublin:
    Irish Children's Book Trust.
Coghlan, V. and C. Keenan (1996) *The Big Guide to Irish Children's Books*,
    Dublin: Irish Children's Book Trust.
Egoff, S., Stubbs, G. and R. Ashley (1996) *Only Connect (Readings on
    Children's Literature)*, (3rd ed.), Oxford: Oxford University Press.
Fahy, J. (1996) 'Teenage fiction.' In: Coghlan, V. and C. Keenan (1996) *The
    Big Guide to Irish Children's Books*, Dublin: Irish Children's Book
    Trust.
Kiberd, D. (1996) *Inventing Ireland: The Literature of the Modern Nation*,
    London: Vintage/Ebury.

Part 3

Teaching writing

8

Teaching students how to write correct English

Robert Mohr

In chapter 2, Brian Cox uses the word 'craft' in regard to writing. I seized upon the word because with it he hit the nail on the head: writing is a craft. Like every craft, writing has its conventions, its rules and tools, its techniques that have been refined over generations. Like every craft, writing demands a period of apprenticeship, during which an apprentice deliberately learns each step in the process of making something, practises that step until it is sure, and eventually achieves mastery as all the steps in the process come together in the particular eloquence of the craft. Writing is one of the supreme crafts, an artifice which displays our natural human genius for using language beautifully and precisely.

I maintain that writing can be taught and consciously learned as a craft. It has a general principle of organisation that unites its smallest structure to its largest form. It has particular grammatically based structures which have specific purposes and joining techniques. These structures can be defined, demonstrated, and practised as a student writer works towards mastery over the whole task, which is no less a challenge than turning a sphere into a line. It is the line with which a writer works, so I further assert, 'The person who has complete control of the sentence – a line – has overall control in writing'. I say this thinking of the general principle of organisation: 'As in the sentence, so in the paragraph, so in the whole essay'.

As in the sentence, so in the paragraph, so in the whole essay

To demonstrate this principle, I shall consider one writing activity, *coordination*, and show how coordination works in the sentence, in the paragraph, and in the essay. First, however, I should lay a foundation that is a prerequisite for the student's understanding of coordination.

All writing is made of phrases and clauses. A *phrase* is simply a word or group of words. The different phrases derive from the eight parts of speech – noun, pronoun, adjective, verb, adverb, preposition, conjunction, interjection. I would add the article: *the*, *a*, *an*. Phrases are basic grammatical materials from which we build a syntax. They are essential to any composing even though they do not, in their grammatical definition, show anyone how to use them. They must be applied, put to the purpose of composition, worked. Yet to work them, students need to know their definition more consciously than they do when they speak in everyday conversation. I think that by the end of primary education, a student should have a good working knowledge of the parts of speech – a phrasal knowledge – and be able to put the parts to work in basic descriptions and narratives.

The term *clause*, of course, separates first into the independent and dependent types. Students need clearly to understand the three elements of an independent clause, for it contains the core of the sentence. It must:

- contain a subject (a noun or pronoun with a specific function: it should be both the logical and grammatical focus of the clause);
- contain a properly conjugated verb (agree with the subject in person and number; clearly placed in a tense);
- express a complete thought.

The dependent clause has the same first two elements, a subject and verb, but it does not express a complete thought. It is dependent upon an independent clause to finish its thought. Furthermore, its content is subordinate to – less important than – the content in the independent clause to which it is attached. That point unfolds into an important writing unit in itself. There are three kinds of dependent clauses, each of which generates a lesson:

- the adverb clause;
- the adjective (relative) clause; and
- the noun clause.

These clause structures are advanced forms and should be taught later in a course, for a student needs time to practise and absorb each in turn. Still, it helps if the the broader terrain is flagged early, so students know that these kinds of clauses do exist and loom on the horizon.

Once the phrase and the clause have been defined and distinguished from one another, even if sketchily at first, the student needs to develop an acute sense of the core of the independent clause – the subject and its verb. The core is the foundation of any sentence.

CORE = subject + verb in an independent clause

Everything is joined to the core, either directly to the subject or to the verb, or to something else that in turn is joined to the subject or verb. Nothing can be left dangling; everything must be joined properly into the fabric of the sentence and finally attached to its core.

Since the core is so important, it needs magnification. At this point writing instruction takes up the topic of *focus* in the sentence, which includes such concerns as:

- preferring human and concrete subjects to abstract ones;
- making the grammatical subject the same as the logical subject;
- finding accurate, active verbs;
- knowing the uses and abuses of the passive voice.

Focus in the paragraph and essay falls conveniently into place here, especially if students are given the general principle of organisation. They both open up as mini-units.

Once phrase and clause have been defined and the *sentence core* has been clarified – topics which are passed over very briefly here (see Mohr, 1998) – the first real business of composition emerges: joining. While writing is made of structures, the writing process entails the joining of structures.

At this point I shall return to the task of considering the role of coordination in writing.

Coordinating statements

The concept of coordination runs throughout writing. It is fundamental to phrase and clause joining, to paragraph organisation, to essay organisation. In fact, it is one of the three main elements constituting the general principle of organisation.

The dictionary provides an illuminating definition of the term coordinate:

1. To organise diverse elements in a harmonious operation.
2. To place (things) in the same class or order.
3. To balance two equal weights either side of a centre point.

Coordination in the sentence

Coordination at the sentence level requires balancing and joining items like grammatical structures that have equal weight or importance. This joining is done through the coordinating conjunctions.

The seven coordinating conjunctions:

		memory aid:
and	f	for
but	a	and
yet	n	nor
so	b	but
or	o	or
for	y	yet
nor	s	so

I recommend that students memorise the seven coordinating conjunctions as a discrete group so that they can always distinguish them from other kinds of conjunctions which may have similar meanings but very different functions. For instance, 'but' and 'although' both express opposition, yet they are different kinds of conjunctions and have very different effects upon the clauses to which they are prefixed. 'But' coordinates two equally weighted, independent clauses while 'although' subordinates a dependent clause to an independent clause. The two conjunctions, one coordinating, the other subordinating, function differently in the sentence.

Two purposes of coordinating conjunctions

1. Coordinating conjunctions introduce and join coordinate clauses:

All seven coordinating conjunctions can join independent clauses (sentences) and, in so doing, give equal emphasis to each clause and express the logical relationship between the ideas in those sentences.

(logical relationship)

1. Sean learned CPR, and his brother followed his example.   (addition)
2. Clare and Sinéad took a computer programming course, but Sinéad couldn't tolerate the hours in front of the monitor.   (opposition)
3. I wanted to finish my report that evening, yet the library closed early on Fridays.   (opposition)
4. We needed to get to the theatre on time, so I rang for a taxi.   (cause-effect)
5. You must print out another copy, or we will have to share this one.   (alternative)
6. He printed another copy, for they didn't want to share the one.   (effect-cause)
7. The audience didn't like the speaker, nor did the speaker care for the audience.   (negative addition)

2. Coordinating conjunctions join phrases:

Four of the coordinating conjunctions – and, or, but, yet – can join elements within the sentence. They:

- join subjects: William or Edel requested the report.

- join verbs: Edel requested the report but rejected its recommendations.

- join direct objects: The staff wanted a new copying machine and a better coffee maker.

- join prepositional phrases: He filed the report in the right filing cabinet yet in the wrong folder.

Three reasons for learning these seven coordinating conjunctions as a group:

1. The parts they join together are of equal importance in the sentence; they balance equally weighted thought; they coordinate.

2. When a coordinating conjunction joins two complete sentences, we normally put a comma between the two independent clauses and in front of the coordinator. We do not necessarily do this with subordinating conjunctions.

3. Unlike other joining words, the coordinators can introduce single-clause sentences and thus serve also as transition words. This is true because, when a coordinating conjunction attaches to an independent clause, it does not make that clause an incomplete thought or a dependent clause. The single clause retains its independent status; it remains a complete thought; it is still a sentence in itself. I recommend that people look at the work of their favourite writers to see whether they in fact do start sentences with *and, or, yet, but,* etc. (Given objections, I cite Fowler, *A Dictionary of Modern English Usage,* 2nd edn, p. 29, entry on *and,* no. 5.)

    Each of the example sentences (on p. 85) could have been written as two complete and separate sentences:

1. Sean learned CPR. And his brother followed his example.

2. Clare and Sinéad took a computer programming course. But Sinéad couldn't tolerate the hours in front of the monitor.

3. I wanted to finish my report. Yet the library closed early on Fridays.

4. We needed to get to the theatre on time. So I rang for a taxi.

5. You must print out another copy. Or we will have to share this one.

6. He printed another copy. For they didn't want to share the one.

7. The audience didn't like the speaker. Nor did the speaker care for the audience.

A writer separates and punctuates in this way to give greater emphasis to the ideas. If the ideas do not deserve such emphasis, the clauses should be joined rather than separated, or the conjunction should be removed from the front of the second clause.

As a rule of thumb, one should not begin more than two sentences within any paragraph with a coordinating conjunction, and this certainly not in successive paragraphs. It should be saved for emphasis. And emphasis loses its impact if it gets placed too often. The practice of placing coordinating conjunctions at the beginning of sentences can easily become a stylistic habit. They draw attention to themselves in that position and the reader notices and gets distracted. It is like a speaker using the same emphatic hand gesture repeatedly during a speech. Soon people in the audience begin to count and stop listening.

Two of the coordinators – *so* and *yet* – can be used a little differently from the others. They can be used together with the coordinator *and* to make a two-word coordinator – *and so* and *and yet*:

I needed a break, *and* so my boss sent me on a holiday to rest.

There was no reason for a war to take place, *and yet* they went into battle wilfully.

The meaning does not change when one adds the *and* to *so* or *yet*. The tone becomes a little more conversational, but that is the only difference. In formal writing and speaking this conversational tone is usually inappropriate, so one must use discretion.

Coordinate sequence paragraph

The general principle of organisation holds that the sentence and the paragraph share structural features. For instance, a writer not only keeps sentence focus clear by placing the logical subject (what the sentence is about) in the grammatical subject position, but also keeps a paragraph coherent by linking the sentence subjects directly to the topic.

Sentences and paragraphs share another structural parallel in the idea of coordination. Just as clauses of equal importance can be joined together into sentences by the coordinating conjunctions, so too can paragraphs be built out of a series of equally weighted sentences, each kept on the same level of generality, each linked directly to the topic sentence: the 'coordinate sequence paragraph' (Christensen, 1967).

These paragraphs tend to be like lists, sometimes referred to as the 'shopping-list' paragraph; they work well as introductions. Each sentence in a coordinate sequence introductory paragraph can itself act as a topic sentence controlling a whole paragraph and very likely will do so in the body of an essay or a report. These paragraphs also work as summations within the body of an essay, and as conclusions. Here is an introductory paragraph that is a deliberate list. The subject/subject group in the sentences that follow the topic sentence are emphasised in bold type in order to show how each sentence links to the first one and to highlight the focus which the authors deliberately maintain.

> **The objectives of this book** are threefold. First, **it** attempts to describe the overall business environment in Ireland in terms of the business structure, the business environment and the role of the state in industrial development. Second, **it** looks at the four primary industry sectors, namely Traditional, Resource-based, Modern and Services. Third, **the book** attempts to describe the nature of business strategy in the Irish context in terms of strategy formulation and implementation. (Lynch and Roche, 1995)

The list-like scheme of this paragraph is clear as it stands. Nevertheless, if we rank each sentence according to its level of generality – the most general being no. 1, and the next more specific being no. 2 – we can chart graphically how the sentences each develop directly out of the topic sentence.

1 The objectives of this book are threefold.

2   First, it attempts to describe the overall business environment in Ireland in terms of the business structure, the business environment and the role of the state in industrial development.

2   Second, it looks at the four primary industry sectors, namely Traditional, Resource-based, Modern and Services.

2   Third, the book attempts to describe the nature of business strategy in the Irish context in terms of strategy formulation and implementation.

In its barest outline, this would look as follows:

1

2

2

2

The next paragraph is also a list, yet of a different sort. Here all of the subjects/subject groups are different from one another. Still, each represents an item we can imagine in 'the Arab market' and this provides the linkage that holds the paragraph together.

The Arab market in Jerusalem is like a scene out of Arabian Nights. **Children** peek timidly around corners and disappear into dark stairwells. **A fat rat** struggles down the gutter and savagely attacks a piece of bread crust. **Scents of hashish with shish kebab and thick waves of smoke** stagnate above the market in the still heat. **The harrowing sound of Islamic bells** echoes through the streets several times a day accompanied by harmonious voices waiting in prayer. From early morning until sunset, **people** bargain for items such as clothing, jewellery, food products, live animals, and Middle-Eastern souvenirs. **Old men** sit in the dust playing backgammon, drinking thick, sweet coffee. **Donkeys and goats** wander wearily through the market. And in the sweet shops, **honey and almond candies** are piled high to the ceiling like bricks in a pyramid. (author unknown)

The next paragraph is an introductory paragraph, the first in the book from which it is taken. It is an overture to the whole book and, therefore, contains elements of the book's themes, each of which must be unfolded in the chapters and paragraphs which follow. The list-like structure is simple, yet the paragraph carries a great wealth of suggestive material. One senses that the superstructure needs to be simple so that it is strong enough to carry the load of the list. Nevertheless, each sentence centres upon the image of O'Brien as pioneer – an image presented in the opening sentence of the paragraph and reinforced in every subsequent statement.

> **Kate O'Brien** is a pioneer. **She** is the first writer of Irish fiction to represent fully and meticulously the Catholic upper-middle class. And **her innovation** goes further [a transition or linking statement]. **She** is the first to address issues common among Irish women of the twentieth century and to introduce into Irish literature questions of female autonomy, self-definition, and sexual freedom that current writers, such as Edna O'Brien, Julia O'Faolain, and Val Mulkerns continue to address. Further still, **she** tenders the earliest female version of the Irish artistic quest that serves as a compelling analogue to the masculine experience explored initially by James Joyce, in *A Portrait of the Artist as a Young Man*, and later by such writers as Sean O'Faolain, in *Birds Alone*, and John McGahern, in *The Dark*. And finally, as deeply committed to Ireland as any of her male literary colleagues, residents and expatriates alike, **Kate O'Brien** scrutinises, even from long distance, the dominant social and political problems that beset her homeland. As do many of her male contemporaries, **she** consistently portrays the land and 'mentalité' she sought to escape. But **Kate O'Brien's Ireland** differs profoundly from theirs, and her singular perspective warrants a prominent place in Irish letters. (Dalsimer, 1990)

Coordinate sequence essay

Now I shall address the structure of an essay in light of the general principle of organisation and the practice of coordination. As a sentence has a core plus additions and a paragraph has a topic sentence plus development sentences, so an essay has a thesis assertion which is developed by the topic sentences which ensue. The topic sentences can be set in a sequence of coordinate levels, in a sequence of subordinate levels, or, as is most practised, in mixed-level sequence. In the coordinate sequence, every topic sentence derives directly from the thesis statement. In this way an essay too can appear as a list.

At one time student writers were taught the 'five-paragraph' essay form. It is actually a coordinate sequence essay whose first paragraph introduces the subject and makes an assertion in the thesis statement. Three paragraphs follow, each headed by a topic sentence that derives directly from the thesis statement: point one, two, three. The essay concludes with a restatement of the thesis, informed and substantiated by the points in the argument, perhaps carrying a persuasive punch. It resembles musical sonata form – ABA – and apprentice writers have been exhorted to use the structure to 'tell them what you want to tell them, tell them, and then tell them what you told them'. This sounds facetious, yet it clarifies in crude terms what an essay does. Such a structure provides a simple, manageable format that serves in a timed essay examination when the writer is put under pressure to produce an essay quickly.

While the idea of the coordinate sequence essay sounds simple, in the hands of a skilled writer it can appear rich and complex. A classic example of this structure, E.M. Forster's 'My Wood', develops the 'five-paragraph essay' into a gem. While I cannot reproduce the whole essay here (see Mohr, 1998: 87–90), I can present the thesis statement, topic sentences, and barest portion of the conclusion so that you can see the scaffolding of its carefully coordinated structure.

My Wood

Paragraph 1. Thesis statement: What is the effect of property upon the character? . . . If you own things, what's their effect on you? What's the effect on me of my wood?

Paragraph 2. Topic sentence: In the first place, it makes me feel heavy.

Paragraph 3. Topic sentence: In the second place, it makes me feel it ought to be larger.

Paragraph 4. Topic sentence: In the third place, property makes its owner feel that he ought to do something to it. Yet he isn't sure what.

Paragraph 5. Topic sentence: And this brings us to our fourth and final point: the blackberries.

Paragraph 6. Conclusion: And perhaps I shall come to this in time. I shall wall in and fence out until I really taste the sweets of property.

As you read the essay, you do not notice Forster's obvious bench marks: 'in the first place . . . in the second place . . . in the third place . . . fourth and final point'. The essay is so full of self-critical humour and rich imagery that the reader does not register the devices. Yet they are there to be seen in skeletal form. He shows us that a simple, coordinated structure can still show wit.

Conclusion

The simplest kind of joining – coordination – is fundamental to writing. Without it a writer could not put two phrases together, could not balance thought, could not show many equal facets of a complex subject. And it provides the first real step forward in joining. After a writer has some control over coordination in its three dimensions – the sentence, the paragraph, the essay – that person is ready for the next kind of joining, subordination, with all its implications and conventions. These structures require skill which develops with practice, and the skills intermingle with seemingly infinite variety as do the seven notes in the musical scale.

References

Christensen, F. (1967) 'A generative rhetoric of the sentence.' In: *Notes Toward a New Rhetoric*, New York: Harper & Row.

Dalsimer, A.M. (1990) 'Preface.' In: *Kate O'Brien, A Critical Study*, Dublin: Gill & Macmillan.

Forster, E.M. (1936/1964) 'My wood.' In *Abinger Harvest*, New York: Harcourt Brace Jovanovich.

Lynch, J.J.and F.W. Roche (1995) *Business Management in Ireland*, Dublin: Oak Tree Press.

Mohr R. (1998) *How to Write: Tools for the Craft*, Dublin: University College Dublin Press.

Exercises in the use of coordinating conjunctions

I. Using coordinating conjunctions, students join the following sentences. They also should indicate the logical relationship between the two independent clauses. In these exercises, there are many short examples taken from a variety of situations, so students can repeatedly use the conjunctions in different contexts. Like five-finger exercises, their repetition gives the student an automatic facility.

logic

1. I play the piano. My sister sings. _____

2. You can work on your proposal.
   We can have a meeting. _____

3. I don't have enough information for my report.
   What I have is not very useful. _____

4. I voted for the man. I still don't like him. _____

5. He took the course twice. He may have to
   take it a third time. _____

6. I hope you'll visit us again soon.
   We always enjoy seeing you. _____

7. I am not going to quit my job. I shall
   not ask for a promotion. _____

8. The company had over-extended its resources.
   The Board recommended cutting expenses. _____

[Suggested answers: and, or, nor, but/yet, and/yet, for, nor, so]

II. What is wrong with the conjunctions in these sentences? Can you substitute more correct ones?

1. Sharon always arrives on time, and Janet frequently shows up late.

2. We can proceed as we always have, but you can propose an alternative plan.

3. The book's binding got dented, so it fell off the table.

4. The furniture is very worn, so the carpets need replacing.

5. The temperature dropped too quickly, and the glass cracked.

6. I found the document that I was looking for, and the print was too small to read.

[Suggested answers: but/yet, or, for, and, so, but]

III. Further joining: Using coordinating conjunctions, join the following sentences. Also indicate the logical relationship between the two independent clauses.

logic

1. There was a thick fog. He had great difficulty finding his way. _____

2. Joseph shouted out. Nobody heard him. _____

3. He tried to swim to shore. His clothes dragged him down. _____

4. Henry had a hard head. Edward had a soft heart. _____

5. The trainer handed him a new hurley. He began to play much better. _____

6. At the same moment the rain poured down. The sun shone through a break in the clouds. _____

7. The fire brigade arrived in ten minutes. It was then too late. _____

8. The storm blew down the tree next to the house. It crashed through the roof. (cause–effect) _____

9. He did not wear an overcoat. He did not carry an umbrella. _____

10. I felt quite happy. My proposal had been accepted by the committee. _____

11. The director arrived late. The meeting was cancelled. _____

12. The road was clear. The crew had worked quickly. _____

13. No train ran that day. No bus did either. _____

14. The train stopped. The people got out. _____

15. Jill looked for her lost book. She could not find it. _____

16. We hoped to go out for a walk. The weather was fine. _____

17. They had to hurry to the station. Their friend would miss his train. _____

[Suggested answers: 1–so, 2–yet/but, 3–but, 4–and/but, 5–so, 6–and, 7–but, 8–so/and, 9–nor, 10–for, 11–so, 12–for, 13–nor, 14–so/and, 15–but, 16–for, 17–or]

Summary of the logical relationships expressed by the seven coordinating conjunctions

CONJUNCTION	LOGICAL RELATIONSHIP
AND	INDICATES ADDITION His job brought in several thousand pounds a month [one source of his money], *and* he got another large sum from an inheritance [a second source].
BUT	INDICATES OPPOSITION/CONTRAST She got the job she wanted, *but* it required that she commute farther.
YET	We enjoyed the concert, yet many others complained about its length
SO	INDICATES CAUSE–EFFECT She convinced the committee, [cause] *so* it adopted her proposal. [effect]
OR	INDICATES ALTERNATIVE She will have to find a new job, *or* her family will go mad. To be *or* not to be. That is the question
FOR	INDICATES EFFECT–CAUSE Charlie had to type the whole essay again, [effect] *for* his computer inexplicably erased the original. [cause]
NOR	INDICATES NEGATIVE ADDITION They could find no fault in the system, nor did any signs of stress appear on the surface.

9

Teaching discursive writing in the senior cycle
John Devitt

On a sultry July afternoon many years ago when I was marking Leaving Certificate Higher Level scripts in the tiny upstairs bedroom which serves as an office, my wife called me down to the kitchen for a cup of coffee. We exchanged a few desultory remarks across the table and then, no doubt to fill a gap in the conversation, she asked the very reasonable question: 'What was the last essay you read about?' I started to answer but found to my surprise that I could not say. My wife was at first incredulous, then amused, finally scandalised. My reaction was different. I knew that I had been reading scrupulously and sympathetically, observing the guidelines provided by the chief inspector at the plenary conference of examiners only a week or two earlier. When my initial embarrassment had worn off, I was able to review the situation with a clear conscience. I could safely assume that the candidate had written diligently and with a considerable investment of youthful energy. Why, then, had an attentive reading of a conscientious piece of writing produced such a very evanescent effect on my consciousness?

Style and effect

It was a defining moment for me. I began to examine my own responses to the scripts I was reading. I began to speculate on why so many otherwise excellent candidates had failed to do themselves justice in the writing of an essay *on a topic of their own choosing*. I compiled a list of recurring and damaging defects in essay-writing with a view to attempting a general diagnosis and suggesting to my colleagues in the Association of Teachers of English possible pedagogical treatment. It is true that many of the items on my list had been anticipated by that wise old owl, the chief inspector, but some had not. Later in this piece, I will return to the list, but I want first of all to underline the implications of my opening anecdote before it is forgotten. We might all agree on this much: every essay, indeed every piece of writing of whatever sort, ought to produce some effect on the reader, not necessarily a lasting effect but certainly not a momentary one. A good essay persuades the reader to speculate about the subject or the writer's treatment of the subject. A really excellent essay produces some such effect but it provides something more: it communicates to those with an educated sensitivity to language a glow of pleasure in the formal and stylistic excellence of the writing. No reasonable examiner demands intellectual profundity allied to formal perfection from candidates working under intense pressure in an examination hall but I would be reluctant to award the highest grades to essays which did not offer, at least intermittently, some of the satisfactions and gratifications I have indicated. The depressing fact is that most of the essays I read during my long stint as an examiner did not invite any such positive discrimination. On the contrary! Terms like 'routine', 'anodyne', 'unexceptionable', 'lifeless' and 'uninteresting' were frequently inscribed in the margins.

It might reasonably be objected that my experience is hopelessly irrelevant. After all, I have not taught at second level since 1979 and my first-hand knowledge of the performance of Leaving Certificate candidates is almost equally out of date. I wish I felt that what follows is of purely historical interest, a catalogue of vices long since eradicated. But the evidence available to me suggests otherwise. Colleagues in my own institution as well as in other colleges of education, not to speak of the universities, are concerned and sometimes appalled by the almost universal failure

of their students to write a serviceable prose. And these are
students, remember, with very creditable grades in the Leaving
Certificate, students who are eloquent or at least vocal in tutorials
and are genuinely interested in the courses they are pursuing.
Some educators blame the *Zeitgeist*, point to the greatly increased
retention rate at second and third levels, and conclude that the
process of deterioration is both inevitable and irreversible. I do
not propose to take refuge in such genteel despair. But perhaps
Hardy was right when he wrote in an ironical and metaphysical
vein: 'if way to the Better there be it exacts a full look at the
Worst'. I propose now to consider in some detail what goes wrong
when students in their late teens put pen to paper.

Common difficulties

Some essays are so inaccurately and unidiomatically written that
even the most sympathetic reader finds it impossible to focus on
what is being said; the mode of expression is so defective that it
usurps the attention. While this may seem like an extreme case,
it is by no means unusual. Again, some essays are largely irrelevant, though rarely if ever completely so, a fact registered at all
examiners' conferences I have attended. It is common enough for
agitated essayists to recognise belatedly that much of what they
have written is beside the point and there is a kind of sardonic
amusement to be derived from observing their awkward attempts
to recover lost ground. Similarity of sentence length and sentence
structure is frequently encountered; a dozen or more sentences in
a short essay may have the same or similar opening phrases. The
effect, of course, is soporific. I should add that some sentences
wander all over the page in search of a full stop and part company
with any meaning they might have had in the writer's mind when
they were first conceived. Equally distressing to the reader is the
persistent use of one manner or mode: an essay may well consist
entirely of generalised assertion without evidence or argument; or
it might consist entirely of description or narration or dialogue.
I might note here the prevalence of a sort of colloquial style,
with all the repetitiousness and syntactical incompleteness which
is admissible in conversation but unwelcome on the page.
   Paragraphing is a lost art, it seems. Some essays consist of a
succession of single-sentence paragraphs of the type beloved by

tabloid journalists who are determined not to overestimate the powers of concentration of their readers. On the other hand, it is common enough to find paragraphs which are essay-length, as if the writer had switched on the automatic pilot, or was mesmerised by the words flowing from his or her pen and powerless before them. The failure to paragraph intelligently is an infallible index of a deeply rooted failure to recognise how an idea needs to be developed, illustrated, qualified and, if need be, challenged. It is not surprising that so many essays end unsatisfactorily, as if sheer exhaustion decreed the final full stop. Some essays end abruptly, often at the bottom of a page; the reader optimistically turns over a new leaf only to be confronted by a blank expanse of virgin paper. Others end with pompous generalisations which are unconvincing because unearned. Probably a majority of the essays I read as an examiner at Leaving Certificate ended with a trite, laborious and unnecessary summary: 'Thus we see from what I have already said . . .'

What startled me most, however, was the frequency with which I encountered unacknowledged contradictions. It takes perhaps seven or eight minutes for an examiner to read an essay on which a candidate has worked for an hour or more; contradictions hidden from the writer are cruelly obvious to the reader. Some of the contradictions may represent cunning attempts by the writer to retreat from an untenable position or to curry favour with the examiner. But I am convinced that the vast majority of them are quite unconscious. Nothing is more damaging to an essay, especially one which mounts some sort of argument, than unacknowledged self-contradiction; it does violence to the reader's expectations. One might conclude that such writers cannot think, or do not know what they think, or have no personal convictions. On a bad day one might even suppose that their mental equipment has been damaged by their educational experience. It is a strange business, however we explain it.

I have said nothing about poor spelling and punctuation, which are frequently and loudly complained of, though all writers of English find such matters difficult and problematic. We should extend a certain latitude to our students, if only in the hope of being forgiven for our own lapses and eccentricities. It would surprise me if all who read this piece could confidently spell, even at this late date in our century, the word 'millennium'. How many hoteliers offer excellent accommodation and spell 'accommodation' wrongly on their letterheads?

I could go on but perhaps I have said enough about what goes wrong when young people write for you to confess yourselves baffled as to what teachers might do about these problems. If we were to attend individually and sequentially to all the vices of style and expression that I have identified there would be time for little else under the rubric of English. Furthermore, it is difficult to see how such a pedagogical approach could be made interesting. English would become synonymous with dullness if teachers proceeded with uniform motion along a straight line towards the goal of accurate expression. Besides, that is not how we learn anything at all, anything we value. We learn in sudden surges of emotional and intellectual excitement or we are driven to learn by the discovery of some pressing need. Learning grows out of learning; one kind of achieved mastery prompts us to attempt another. There ought to be a pedagogical equivalent of Ockham's razor, a principle of economy in teaching and learning, adherence to which permits us to attend simultaneously to a multitude of concerns. Where the teaching of writing is concerned such an instrument exists: we might call it the interrogative method.

Writing from an interrogative stance

I propose to leave aside for the moment the question of how an essay might begin and the question of how an essay might end – two questions which are really one, as we shall see. If you review the list of dangerous and damaging defects I have just worked through, you will see that most of them are the inevitable result of poor preparation or no preparation at all. I am not recommending that young students should be encouraged to spend a large amount of time on the construction of colour-coded spider diagrams or in writing massive quantities of notes. I want to suggest a much more economical method of generating and organising ideas, one that is simple, practicable and memorable. Not the least of the advantages I would claim for this method is that it relieves anxiety and involves on the part of teachers and learners an act of confidence in the power of the human mind. (Some of us are old enough to remember when education used to concern itself with developing that power.) We all have the ability to raise questions, our own questions. Good questions have two properties which are relevant here: in the first place they may suggest answers, at least in outline, or send us in the right direction; in the second place, good questions are invariably pregnant with other, perhaps better, questions. The ability to think interrogatively, to question what is taken for granted, to problematise routine responses, ought to be fostered and the right place to foster it is in the English class when students are being taught to write.

I want you to imagine a teacher in some classroom in Dublin proposing to a group of teenagers a topic for an essay. Let the theme be as hackneyed as you will: 'Loneliness', perhaps, or 'World War Three', or 'God made the country, man made the town', or 'The shape of things to come', or 'Time will tell', or 'The Freedom of the Press'. (I will not say which of these topics appeared on last year's Leaving Certificate Higher Level paper, for that is not important.) I want you to imagine the teacher making a slightly unexpected move. Instead of saying: 'Write an essay of c.1000 words on the topic of your choice', he or she invites the class to address nine or ten questions to one topic. What is loneliness? Is it curable? Or a necessary part of being human? Is it commoner now than formerly? If so, why so? Is loneliness an urban or a rural complaint? Is it the same as being alone? What are the most evocative images of loneliness, in song, in poetry, in fiction, in film, or in drama? Are young people lonelier than their parents? What's it like to be lonely? Can it be identified by observation? Or is it above all a condition known only through experience? Now the teacher invites the class to critique the questions they have come up with, to eliminate those that are obviously tedious or uninteresting, and to number those that remain in the order they might attack them in an essay. It will be enough in the way of homework for the students to order their questions and perhaps to write a single paragraph in response to one of them. In a day or two they might read these paragraphs aloud to the class and discuss each other's work.

This, it seems to me, is a way of generating and organising ideas that any pupil of average ability can master with a modicum of practice. It has a number of incomparable advantages. It proposes that young people should take pleasure in the exercise of their God-given abilities. It enables them to discover their own imaginative power. It is consistent with their self-respect and diminishes their depressing dependency on their teacher. Intellectual life begins with questioning and knows no end. The process has obvious political and economic implications: those who are schooled in this method are unlikely to be subservient to their political masters or easily manipulated by commercial interests. But the merely prosaic advantages of the method are worth reciting. It is so simple that it cannot be forgotten even in the stressful context of the certificate examinations. It does not prescribe what writers must write but liberates them into the discovery of what they have it in them to say. It is a genuinely heuristic method which can be applied to any topic at any level – would that postgraduate dissertations were so ordered. No one who uses this method will be in any doubt as to what constitutes a paragraph: a paragraph is simply the formed response to a question. If the ordering of questions is done intelligently, then the resultant essay will have the kind of structure that makes self-contradiction and irrelevance highly unlikely, if not impossible.

And there are two other advantages, admittedly shared with all other methods of preparation even those which are far more elaborate and time-consuming. If inspiration is granted by a fickle Muse, the method can be laid aside quietly. This is a rare occurrence, though it should not be ruled out. Writing is for the most part a series of deliberate choices, a process as strenuous as it is rewarding, as demanding as it is fulfilling. But every now and again we write a prose that surprises us, that has a singing quality we delight in without knowing its mysterious source. Such writing is God's gift to those who have laboured long and hard. The final advantage which attaches to any useful method of preparation is this: it enables the writer to concentrate on the act of writing itself. Bad writing is the product of a distracted, anxious and divided mind. When you do not know what the substance of your next paragraph is going to be, your syntax is likely to disintegrate, your spelling to deteriorate, your phrasing to become awkward and unidiomatic. With an enabling structure in mind, young essayists can attend to the detail of their writing; they might ensure that every paragraph contains at least one very short sentence, of no more than six or eight words. The short sentence represents a welcome commitment to clarity. Furthermore, they might have sufficient leisure to avoid the banal repetition of word and phrase which suggests a restricted vocabulary. I recommend this principle of economy to teachers for I know from experience that it works very well. It does not solve all problems but it does reduce their number to more manageable proportions.

I want to consider briefly one problem I postponed – that of beginnings and endings. There is in fact an infinite number of ways of beginning an essay. You might start with an anecdote, a definition, a description, a fragment of dialogue, an exemplum, an assertion, a quotation, an autobiographical detail, a rhetorical flourish, a visionary excursion to some hell or heaven of the imagination. It is no matter – provided that you are prepared to live with the consequences. In practice, this means that the concluding paragraph should echo the opening paragraph to some perceptible degree. This is the best way to communicate the sense of an ending to the reader. Of course, a concluding paragraph can also open up new vistas, new possibilities, by a measured departure to another point of view; having said what you set out to say, you end by indicating your awareness of other fruitful approaches. All this may be done briefly: the final paragraph should be significantly shorter than the average length of your other paragraphs. That is how you provoke your reader into the kind of speculation a good essay should stimulate.

Widening the frame

I want to widen the frame for a moment, by relating the activity of writing to the other activities which go on in the English class. In recent years we have been asked to think in terms of an integrated curriculum, in which reading, writing, listening and talking flow into and out of each other. The idea is supposed to be a revolutionary one, though it was common practice in the sixties. Nevertheless it is still worth asserting and reflecting on. For one thing it gives to English an identity and an integrity which was called into question by at least one minister for education, the late Brian Lenihan, who, you will remember, succeeded Donogh O'Malley on the latter's death in 1968. It was the Association of Teachers of English which opposed the minister's proposal to divorce the study of the vernacular language from the study of the vernacular literature. Various GCE boards in Britain actively promoted this thoroughly dysfunctional practice by examining English language and English literature separately. There was a nauseating political notion at work subterraneously, the assumption that members of a certain socio-economic class could not be expected to relish poetry or Shakespeare's plays or Dickens's novels. The cure for their existing deprivation was to be further deprivation. There was a more rational but still specious argument behind Mr Lenihan's proposal. Since in adult life most people are called upon to write business letters, reports, surveys, summaries and the like, it was assumed that the study of highly figurative and stylised literary texts was actually an impediment to the development of a settled, transparent and functional prose. The reverse is the case. Those who have no sensitivity to the literary uses of the vernacular are precisely those whose prose is full of dead or clashing metaphors, unwanted rhymes, barbarous solecisms, silly pomposities and unconscious ambiguities. The clearest, cleanest and most transparent prose written in our century is the work of writers whose inner ear was perfectly attuned to the literary uses of the language, like George Orwell and Hubert Butler.

Towards a theory of writing: ten propositions

At this point, I would like to put forward a series of ten propositions all of which have a bearing on the relationship between writing and the other activities proper to English. I call them propositions not principles, to emphasise their tentative character; none of them is true in all cases and some are superficially at odds with others. In fact, none of these propositions can be mechanically applied. If teaching is an art, as I believe, then the teaching of writing is the most difficult part of the mystery, involving many subtle moves, many carefully calculated interventions, and requiring a whole repertoire of experiments.

I offer these ten propositions to you for critical reflection in the hope that, personally modified in the light of your own experience, they may prove useful.

1. Classroom discussion should precede all written assignments.

2. Writing and speaking are different, though related skills.

3. Prose which cannot be read aloud with clarity and force is likely to be feeble and uninteresting.

4. The variety of forms encountered by pupils in their reading should be reflected in the variety of forms they attempt as writers.

5. Specific instructions about tone, style, length, form and structure should accompany every written assignment.

6. Written assignments need not be elaborate in form, exhaustive in scope or complete in their execution to be stimulating and useful exercises.

7. No one writes well unless some form of publication is proposed.

8. The information quotient of an essay is not all-important; good writing is tentative, exploratory and imaginative.

9. The crucial determinant of tone is the relationship between the writer and the reader.

10. The inner ear can be educated only by developing skills in the close reading of literary texts.

Perhaps we could now consider some of these propositions, in particular the first three.

Classroom discussion should precede all written assignments: discussion puts ideas and words into circulation, suggests possibilities, awakens memories, clarifies meanings; even those who do not actively participate in such discussion derive considerable benefits as mere silent auditors. I recognise that it may not always be possible to budget for a discussion of every projected essay topic; indeed it may sometimes be deemed undesirable. Nevertheless, structured discussion may encourage those who feel powerless because they have nothing to say, to attack a writing assignment with some degree of optimism and courage.

One of the problems with the idea of an integrated curriculum in English is that it can easily be misunderstood; good writing is not the accurate record of good speech. My second proposition addresses this question: *Writing and speaking are different, though related skills*. We are all familiar with disputants and debaters whose writing skills lag far behind their highly developed oral skills. We know too that the transcript of a conversation is a very different thing from a face-to-face dialogue and, as a general rule, reads badly. To write exactly as one speaks is a fatal mistake. This knowledge should qualify our enthusiasm for classroom discussion as a necessary preliminary to a writing exercise, without altogether invalidating it. There is no golden rule. But perhaps the third proposition will prove helpful: *Prose which cannot be read aloud with clarity and force is likely to be feeble and uninteresting.* If it is true that speech cannot be rendered as writing without losing vitality and clarity, surely the converse is true also: surely writing loses when read aloud? Some years ago I found a creative use for the photocopier: I took copies of essays which I subsequently asked students to read aloud. The extraordinary thing is that, as they read, they corrected defective syntax, restored words which had been inadvertently eliminated in the writing, and skipped over unnecessary repetitions of word and phrase; they paid much closer attention to rhythm and tone than might have been expected. In short, they became educable, they became sensitive critics of their own prose performances. Outside of the Oxbridge tutorial system, such refinements of the art of teaching are simply not practicable on a regular basis. But perhaps something of the sort can be done occasionally even in our crowded classrooms, by breaking the class into small groups, for example.

It is not absurd to require students in the senior cycle of our schools to write essays, though there is something absurd about feeling constrained to defend the practice. For the labour of preparation, the very business of writing and rewriting, and the subsequent review of one's own essay in the light of the teacher's response are profoundly educational. The essayist engages in that struggle with words and meaning about which Eliot wrote in *Four Quartets*; he or she learns to resist the first, tempting word that offers itself and to search for the *right* word instead. In particular, the young essayist learns that the last word has not been written on any subject whatever, that there is room for his or her own word, and that no one else can write that word. This is an invaluable lesson in self-respect and in citizenship. But it is a lesson that can only be learned with difficulty.

I am not sure of the precise epistemological status of these three propositions, not to speak of the other seven which I do not have space here to gloss. I would not willingly embrace martyrdom for any of them. But they do provide a basis for deliberate, conscious experiment in the classroom, of the type I have adumbrated. By virtue of their explicitness they can be critiqued, refined and developed in the light of experience. When we speak of teaching as an art, we do not mean that it is purely instinctive or intuitive. Neither is it a matter of doing unto others just as was done unto us. Among the likely readership of this paper, I do not need to argue for a pedagogy which is self-conscious, rational, responsible. There are, of course, differences of opinion which need to be registered and explored. Not every teacher of English is as convinced as I am of the importance of essay-writing. Some would argue that the essay is an antiquated form, no longer viable. The disappearance of the old prose anthology which contained essays by Bacon, Lamb, Hazlitt, Stevenson and W.H. Hudson is a sign of the times, or rather a sign of some current educational thinking. I would have to concede that the kinds of essay that anthology contained are not, indeed never were, good models for students, though that is not to say that they cannot be read and studied with profit. The essay is by no means antiquated, however. The leader writers in our newspapers write essays, and so do Nuala O'Faolain, John Waters, Fintan O'Toole, Garret FitzGerald, Declan Kiberd and dozens of others. Why, some of them actually publish collections of essays, on anything and everything. Arguably, no other literary form gives with such fidelity the form and pressure of the time.

A closing thought

I want to return for a moment to that upstairs bedroom, with its malodorous grey sack of pink-covered Leaving Certificate scripts, where I began to reflect seriously on the way our students write. The real scandal is not that I forgot so quickly what I had just read but that so many young people, after ten or twelve years of intensive schooling, could not write well or even tolerably. Something should, something can, be done about it. We need a theory of writing, I would submit, useful in practice but not entirely subservient to practical considerations.

10

Teaching writing skills in the primary school

James Kavanagh

Since the late 1960s and the early 1970s, educationists, researchers and politicians in many developed countries (particularly America) have expressed concern about writing standards among school leavers. Indeed, the 'writing crisis' – a 'crisis' as serious as the infamous 'science crisis' of the 1950s – became an issue in the American press and angry American citizens and politicians criticised the schools for failing in their mission (Furay, 1984). Fortunately, a crisis sometimes can have unexpectedly positive outcomes and it is – at least in part – as a result of the sustained public and political interest which this 'crisis' generated that research into children's writing has undergone something of a revolution in the last 25 years. This is especially true for the United States of America, Canada and Britain.

The outcomes of this revolution have had a profound impact on our understanding of how writing is learnt and how the skills involved in writing well may be taught more effectively. In particular, research findings concerning writing as a *process* as district from a *product*, would seem to have serious implications for practice in Ireland. The *process approach* or *process-conference approach* (as it is more fully known) focuses on the more elusive elements of writing as a composing act (see Graves, 1983). The importance of key aspects of process-conference writing (planning, goal-setting, pre-writing, drafting, revising, and editing) and all the mental processes involved from conception to final production, has long been recognised. Indeed, these have provided the broad thrust of many researchers' work since the pioneering work of Emig (Emig, 1971).

This chapter discusses three aspects of writing instruction at the primary level in contemporary Ireland. The intention of the chapter is to open debate on an important but neglected area of literacy study – the teaching of compositional writing in our primary schools. In the first section, some important findings from international research into the teaching and learning of compositional writing are cited. These usefully set the context for the subsequent discussion of practice and understanding regarding compositional writing in the Irish setting. Section two draws on original research completed in the recent past to present a brief description of the approaches to writing instruction in a sample of Irish primary schools. Necessarily brief, the section nevertheless points to a number of issues of concern uncovered during the research. The final section of the chapter draws some general educational conclusions from the same study and suggests some implications for future development in writing instruction at primary school level in particular. Some of the more salient characteristics of the *process-conference* approach to writing instruction in primary education are noted and its potential advocated.

Compositional writing: what does the research tell us?

The art of writing and the teaching and learning of writing have a long, complicated, circuitous and multi-faceted history. For more than a millennium the art was the preserve of churchmen and an elite group of scribes. The act of composing in writing is a complicated and manifold activity whose intricate mental complexities are only gradually being revealed through research. For children, as developing writers, the task of learning to write is enormous and demanding. They have to learn to control many aspects simultaneously. While there are cross-cultural elements which allow comparison across national cultures and languages, 'good' writing is, by and large, a culturally defined phenomenon in each society. Interventions or developments brought in pupils' writing are really processes of acculturation. In addition, of course, all language curricula which include writing are interwoven with broader goals of education.

Within the context of models of English, models of writing have also been identified. Most prominent among these models is a knowledge-transforming model as opposed to a knowledge-telling model (Bereiter and Scardamalia, 1987). In this model, the act of writing is seen as both natural and problematic: the natural model makes maximum use of the natural human endowments of language competence and of skills learned through ordinary, social experiences but it is also limited by them – and is regarded as a knowledge-telling form of writing. The problematic model, on the other hand, is capable of going beyond the normal linguistic competence in order to enable the writer to accomplish the reprocessing of knowledge and this is known as the knowledge-transforming type of writing. A major distinction between the two models is that knowledge-transforming involves a deliberate strategic control over parts of the process that are unattended to in the more naturally developed version. Users of this form – it is argued – are able to go beyond the ordinary ability to put one's thoughts and knowledge into writing: such competent, skilled or mature writers can shape a piece of writing to achieve intended effects and can reorganise their knowledge in the process.

This model of the composing process has a number of important values. It provides educators with a scheme and a vocabulary to visualise and discuss a complex and ever-changing phenomenon. It also offers an insight into processes and sub-processes and their interchangeability which are available to skilled or competent writers. By identifying the significant differences between adult writers and learner writers or between experts and novices, educators may be in a better position to propose instructional interventions to help novice writers acquire the knowledge and skills of expert and mature writers.

There is some evidence to suggest that skilful writers make use of knowledge of essential forms of various literary genres, e.g. narrative, expository, argumentative, or persuasive kinds of writing; they are said to have knowledge of a discourse scheme (Bereiter and Scardamalia, 1987).

Another significant distinction that emerges in a general way from the literature is that expert writers differ from novice writers in the facility that they bring to the act of writing and in how they use this. For example, in terms of memory searches expert writers appear to differ in two important ways from novice writers. First, the expert can more readily determine the availability of appropriate information in memory rather than simply confining their search patterns to the retrieval of specific items of information. This type of memory enables the writer to avoid dwelling on information about which he/she is unsure but enables him/her to concentrate instead on definite knowledge related to the topic; this type of search is associated with higher level planning skills. Secondly, expert writers engage in more effective goal-directed searches of memory. Essentially, they appear to have the ability to search memory more purposefully and specifically as opposed to haphazardly. Intentional control over language processes may be sufficiently developed to function automatically for mature or skilled writers who thus save mental capacity for use on higher level components of the composing process. For children, on the other hand, it takes extra mental effort to automatise the mechanics of writing. Moreover, what evidence there is suggests that sophisticated writers plan very purposefully by translating high-level goals into sub-goals. In contrast, unpractised writers are much less capable of bringing goals into play explicitly in the planning process and are highly unlikely to operate at the level of sub-goal.

Finally, another crucial difference between skilled and unskilled writers lies in the expert's ability to reprocess text, that is, skilled writers can use text already produced – by themselves or indeed by others – as another input to a further cycle of text processing to transform the original text. This new cycle does not simply add to whatever was produced before but transforms it. Put simply they draft and redraft effectively. This process makes the crucial difference between a knowledge-telling model and a knowledge-transforming model of the composing process. A good picture of this reprocessing approach can be found in Bereiter and Scardamalia (1987) who quote Aldous Huxley's description of the idea in action:

Generally, I write everything many times over. All my thoughts
are second thoughts. And I correct each page a great deal, or
rewrite it several times as I go along . . . Things come to me in
driblets, and when the driblets come I have to work hard to make
them into something coherent. (1987: 10)

In summary, an essential distinction between unskilled or
learner-writers and skilled writers may be described as one of
discursive turn. Learners write the way they do because of the
limited kinds of mental representations of text which they have
available to them. In contrast, skilled writers have flexible access
to a wide range of mental representations of actual and intended
text and of the circumstances influencing plans for that text. As
we shall see in the following section, the conditions under which
writing is often taught in our primary schools would appear to
favour the development of the former rather than the latter.

Writing instruction in Irish primary schools

The author carried out a comprehensive survey of the approaches
to writing instruction in Irish primary schools (Kavanagh, 1998).
The main data gathering instruments used were:

(*a*) postal questionnaires to Second and Sixth class teachers in
134 schools – 274 questionnaires were posted; 188 valid questionnaires were returned which amounts to a valid response rate of
almost 70 per cent;

(*b*) a survey of the writing curricula of trainee-teachers in three
Colleges of Education;

(*c*) an examination of commercial English text books/workbooks;

(*d*) an evaluation of children's writing samples.

Caution must be exercised when generalising results from a
sample of primary teachers to primary teachers in general.
Nevertheless, the returns were felt to offer a reasonably broad and
defensible indication of existing practices and perceptions (see
Kavanagh, 1998). And indeed the findings of the survey indicate
a number of important points about existing practices in writing
instruction in Irish primary classrooms. In particular:

(*a*) the majority of teachers surveyed did not engage in process-
conference approaches to the teaching of writing;

(*b*) teachers allocated a relatively modest amount of time to the teaching of creative writing; more time was allocated to functional writing, mainly in the form of workbook/textbook exercises;

(*c*) most teachers had never taken an in-service course in the teaching of writing;

(*d*) in most cases, teachers assigned the topics for writing for their pupils;

(*e*) pupils practised only a limited range of writing; narrative/ story and descriptive writing were the genres practised most often;

(*f*) teachers did not model the writing process for their pupils;

(*g*) in general, teachers pursued a traditional skills-based approach to the teaching of functional writing;

(*h*) teachers in general pursued a *laissez-faire*, non-involved approach to pupils' creative writing;

(*i*) teachers appeared to rely too much on readers/workbooks as a main source of ideas and stimuli for pupils' writing; the writing mainly involved short answers to literal comprehension questions, the completion of grammar-type exercises and filling-in-the blanks type of drill;

(*j*) two broad categories of writing – creative and functional – were identified; stories/poetry accounted fully for creative writing; functional writing consisted of exercises from class readers, workbooks, book reviews and letters;

(*k*) the making or correcting of pupils' writing by teachers was characterised by identifying misspellings, ticking off, or making encouraging remarks but on no piece of writing was there evidence of comments which actually guided the pupils or pointed to ways in which the writing could be improved;

(*l*) writing curricula in Colleges of Education with one notable exception did not cater adequately for the teaching and learning of writing, either that of the student-teacher or the primary pupil or the academic or professional English courses of the trainee-teachers. Knowledge of writing processes or of the skills of composition seemed to be secondary considerations in the colleges. Relevant courses in the teaching/learning of composition skills have to been provided in the colleges in general. In the absence of specific training, teachers starting their careers are ignorant of the new knowledge and insights in writing instruction.

General educational implications

The general review of the literature and the picture emerging from the above-mentioned survey of writing instruction practices in Irish primary schools raise a number of implications for primary teachers and primary schools in this country.

First, the teacher as master craftsperson must demonstrate the craft of writing. He/she must provide a secure, supportive, predictable and literate classroom for the apprentice-writers. Second, pupils need to be given control over their writing to enable them to choose topics themselves. This has quite significant implications for both the manner and the nature of writing-skills work that takes place in the classroom. (Outlined below – in a basic description of the process-conference approach to writing – is a model that may go some way towards meeting this need.) Third, in-career writing courses are needed for teachers. Teachers should be informed of recent research findings and of models of the teaching of writing. Fourth, more research into the whole area of writing instruction in our schools is required. There is a need for national surveys of pupils' writing abilities over a range of writing genres; there is a need for research which focuses closely on the teaching of writing in classrooms; research is also needed to refine the teaching/learning characteristics of good practice in writing instruction.

In short, we need to look seriously at the idea of radically restructuring the way that we go about teaching writing skills in our primary classrooms and how we go about helping teachers to develop the expertise to do so. It may well be the case that until teachers write and rediscover the writing process for themselves, they will not be able to help their pupils in the ways described in the literature on teaching writing to children. There are strong arguments, then, why we should consider placing a *process-based* view of learning to write at the heart of this 'rediscovery', and in particular what has become known as the *process-conference* approach.

The *process-conference* approach is a relatively new model which views writing as an evolving, organic process. Pieces of writing in the classroom are regarded as growing things which need to be nurtured rather than as objects which need to be repaired or fixed by correction. A number of key characteristics of this approach suggest that it may hold considerable potential for use with learner writers in the primary classroom. These can be articulated as follows:

- The craft of writing is a recursive process; when mature writers work, they engage in a process or craft which includes rehearsal of ideas, drafting, revising and editing.

- Writing and emergent literacy develop together; children know a great deal – albeit rudimentary – about print and its power to convey messages.

- A crucial element of the approach is that the teacher can model the writing process; teachers must demonstrate what writers do and how to do it.

- Writers need real purposes and audiences; writing is not an isolated act in itself; it has a social dimension; pupils should use writing to make, receive and communicate meaning.

- Finally, children's writing develops through the idea of a conference – an ongoing dialogue – between teacher and pupil or master craftsperson and learner (Graves, 1983). This conference serves as a kind of linguistic bridge for children upon which a trusted and knowledgeable adult can provide the child with cues and probes for extended writing. The teacher looks for potential in the words the child speaks or writes in the content of the writing and in the way the pupil approaches the craft of writing.

Researchers have often criticised school writing for being too meaningless to evoke much goal-directed composing or to help develop the type of higher-order writing routines discussed earlier in this chapter (cf. Applebee, 1981; Macrorie, 1976). Good writers focus first on meaning; poor writers who think good writing is merely *correct* writing tend to focus only on correctness and neatness.

The process-conference approach is, arguably, a model for the teaching of writing skills in the primary school which goes a considerable way towards satisfying both the requirement for meaningful engagement with content and structure, and the development of personal writing skills in a truly educative way. In an age when literacy is increasingly important, we would do well to consider its merits.

References

Applebee, A.N. (1981) *Writing in the Secondary School: English and the Content Areas*, Urbana Il: National Council of Teachers of English.

Bereiter, C. and M. Scardamalia (1987) *The Psychology of Written Composition*, New Jersey: Lawrence Erlbaum.

Emig, J. (1971) *The Composition Process of Twelfth Graders*, Urbana Il: National Council of Teachers of English.

Furay, M. (1984) 'The US National Writing Project: a model.' *Rostrum*, 60 (7): 636.

Graves, D. (1983) *Writing: Teachers and Children at Work*, Portsmouth, NH: Heinemann.

Kavanagh, J. (1998) 'A survey of the approaches to the teaching of English compositional writing in a sample of Irish primary schools.' Unpublished PhD thesis, Education Department, UCD.

Macrorie, K. (1976) *Talking Writing*, Rochdale NJ: Hayden.

Part 4

The English curriculum at second level

11

Making it 'real' will make it happen: approaches to literacy development in the new second-level English syllabi

Tom Mullins

In 1712, Jonathan Swift wrote an essay entitled 'A Proposal for Correcting, Improving and Ascertaining the English Tongue', addressed to the Earl of Oxford, The Lord Treasurer of England at that time. In this, in his usual trenchant way, he inveighed against the changes being introduced into the language by what he described as 'university boys' and the 'frequenters of Coffee Houses'. He continued in the following manner:

> My Lord, I do here, in the name of all the learned and Polite Persons of the Nation, complain to your Lordship as First Minister, that our language is extremely imperfect; that its daily improvements are by no means in proportion to its daily Corruptions; that the Pretenders to polish and refine it, have chiefly multiplied Abuses and Absurdities; and that in many instances it offends against every Part of Grammar. (in Crowley, 1991: 28)

I thought it would be useful to begin with this quotation to set the whole debate about standards of literacy and the popular concern about correct usage in an historical setting. It is important to stress that language is a living, cultural entity, subject to permanent change and development in the mouths, pens and computers of its users. It is usage, communicative efficacy, and a relentless simplification of structures and conventions that are the great arbiters of language change. Loud ideological statements, from our poets and writers of quality have little impact on the way language develops. The modern equivalents of 'university boys' and 'frequenters of Coffee Houses' still, happily, multiply Abuses and Absurdities.

Swift's own use of the capital letter in the above extract is a graphic example of the continual change in conventions that occurs in language. To our eyes his usage might be reminiscent of usage now deemed to be incorrect, found in the compositions of some students in schools today that would merit a reprimand from a zealous teacher wielding a red biro.

Language change is inevitable and unstoppable. This offers a challenge to us as educationalists to work out ways of negotiating with that change and managing it in so far as that can be done. The latest news that after two centuries the apostrophe is dying may be offensive to our linguistic sensibilities but it is not a harbinger of a fatal disease in the English language.

Background to second-level syllabi

The two new syllabi in English at second level produced by the National Council for Curriculum and Assessment in the past ten years display a clear remit; they were intended to ensure that the acquisition and study of language were given major emphasis. That remit was the departure point for the relevant syllabus committees to take a fresh look at understanding literacy and also to work out ways in which it could be more convincingly and coherently developed at second level.

The previous syllabi at second level had been based on the traditional assumption that literacy was a linguistic monolith, coterminous with knowledge of Standard English, that could be learnt in a decontextualised, functionalist manner. This led to a situation in which the focus in English had been on achieving what can be called *school literacy* as opposed to real literacy, with the resultant unsatisfactory outcomes that had commentators bewailing the fall off in standards of reading and writing. Although, interestingly enough, according to the Chief Examiner's report on the Higher Level Leaving Certificate 1997, there is no evident lowering of standards, nevertheless there is an evident weakness in higher order critical thinking and linguistic skills.

What do I mean by this phrase *school literacy*? It is best described as an approach to learning language in an artificial way, in what has been described as 'dummy runs'. The ubiquitous presence of the discursive essay form and the semi-mythical place it has established at the centre of teaching and examining English is a good example of this condition. To assume that the ability to write in that one form, usually generalised narrative, for essentially the same audience, in some vague register, was an adequate preparation for the general range of literacy skills and competencies required in society was a false premise. The essay form has its uses but it is not of necessity the royal way to an advanced and flexible literacy.

The same point could be made about decontextualised approaches to the teaching of reading, punctuation and spelling. Students learned to do these exercises, but rarely if ever transferred what they learned to their own real reading and writing. I remember an incident from when I was teaching at second level some years ago and engaging in such literacy development practices. The parents of a student came and said how pleased they were with their son's examination results especially in the area of composition, but could I please explain why his letters home were so appallingly illiterate? Quite clearly my approach was not relating to the real life of the student, and this is the general problem with approaching literacy in this way.

Students emerging from such experiences could be characterised in their attitudes to language as having:

- scant respect for its significance and power in their own lives;

- no understanding of its moral and political importance in society;

- an indifferent attitude to usage in all its forms;

- few perceptions of how language works, i.e. little insight into its structures.

Several literacies to be learned

It was against this background that the new syllabi were conceived and drafted. In response, each syllabus took the stance that the approach to developing literacy had to become more varied and multi-faceted. There was not just one literacy but many literacies to be learnt. Children would have to encounter a range of discourses, both oral and written, which would enable them to take their place in society and to take on the responsibilities of an adult using language in a range of contexts.

Developing such a flexible approach to language development, encouraging students to learn a wide range of discourses, is a significant political act. It places literacy development in a rich framework of social practices and invites students to play their role in our democracy as free, responsible, citizens. It is by putting such a referential frame of values to the fore in the teaching of English that it becomes meaningful and significant for students and gives an enriched moral dimension to the English teacher's role. Developing reading and writing, students must have meaningful experiences, which make the learning of language in all its forms interesting, enriching and stimulating. It is in that way that the power of language will be discovered and a proper attitude of respect developed in students for their own usage.

Any literacy is a social practice, which is given purpose and meaning, by being embedded in values and relationships. Vygotsky commented that children learn language by meaningful negotiation; a young child learns quickly how to call his parents because that is what he/she needs and desires; older students have similar needs and desires that could be the source of much significant negotiation and therefore of literacy development which is integrated and real.

The Junior Certificate syllabus

Putting this vision into practice was the challenge faced by the new syllabi and, in the main, it is fair to say that in aspiration they have been realised. Let us see how they went about trying to achieve these ends.

At Junior Certificate Level, three generic areas of literacy and oracy provided the overarching conceptual structure as follows:

- Personal Literacy – emphasised thinking, fluency and the validity of local language
- Social Literacy – stressed the need to develop formal, functional language
- Cultural Literacy – initiated the students into aesthetic uses of language

Within these three interlinked areas students were expected to develop, in an integrated programme of syllabus units, a wide range of speaking, listening, reading and writing skills.

The person whose work was most influential in the thinking behind the approach to literacy at Junior Certificate level was the late James Britton with his categorisation of language into three broad areas, viz. Expressive, Transactional, Poetic. These are largely identical with the Junior Certificate view of language.

These categories were not to be seen as being mutually exclusive, and could interact significantly in a dialectical manner. Nevertheless they emphasised to students that language use was diverse and multi-faceted and what was appropriate and meaningful in one context was not appropriate in another.

Thus the cultural myth of Standard English and Received Pronunciation as being necessary everywhere and always was put into a proper perspective. Let me be quite clear about this. It is vital that everyone learns Standard English in its written form. A school would be failing in its social responsibility if this aspiration were not given the top priority. Nevertheless it remains true that for a school to insist that Standard English is the only valid version of English, is to fly in the face of linguistic fact and potentially undermine the students' capacity to engage in school and learn in a personally meaningful manner.

Some years ago, I remember supervising a student-teacher who revealed a characteristic and illustrative linguistic attitude. She read a story that included a scene where a parent is angry with a child. Subsequently the teacher asked the class what condition the parent was in and a child blurted out 'Miss, she's burnin' ile'. The teacher commented, 'Yes, Mary, quite right, but it would be better to say, 'the mother is angry. . .'.

I'll leave it to the reader to decide which was the better English here. In the context, give me the metaphor any time with its power and impact. Of course, Standard English has its significant cultural place. It is a literacy of power and prestige and must be given due recognition but not in a way that repudiates other creative literacies which are central and affirming in the lives of our students. However, it needs to be said this does not mean condoning or leaving students locked in a limited personal linguistic base which consists of a mixture of cliches, salacious phrases and soap opera registers. As the Junior Cycle syllabus asserts, 'Diversification and enrichment of a personal linguistic base are the central objectives of the English course at Junior Cycle.' (Department of Education/NCCA 1990: 2)

The structure of the syllabus was carried through into the structure of the examination papers. They have the same tripartite structure and the approach to marking takes due cognisance of the relevant objectives of each section. Thus the concept of literacies remains an integral and liberating concept in all aspects of the Junior Certificate syllabus.

With respect to Oracy the aspiration to give it a larger role remains. The Minister for Education and Science, Mr Micheál Martin, shortly after his appointment in May 1997, indicated that the development of oral programmes and assessment procedures should be given a priority status in the syllabi, and the NCCA English Committees are awaiting further clarification and direction. Oracy is an issue which will require much careful planning particularly in the area of assessment if the best is to be garnered for the students from the introduction of the oral domain. Initially, a Pilot Scheme at Junior Certificate Level would perhaps be the best way to start on this and it is hoped it will not be too long before such is initiated.

The Leaving Certificate syllabus

Moving on to the new Leaving Certificate syllabus, so long in gestation, the same emphasis on real contexts, literacies and the integration of language skills is to be found. But two other perspectives – which were largely implicit in the syllabi up to now – become foregrounded. These are the important areas of Language Awareness and Critical Literacy that add an intellectual sophistication to the perception of language use appropriate for Leaving Certificate students

These two ways of looking at language use provide a stance which permeates the whole syllabus and point to the need for students to understand how language works in any text and, furthermore, to the value systems inherent in all uses of language.

Central to the Leaving Certificate syllabus is the concept of language as a dynamic shaping presence in human experience redolent with cultural values. Students building on their experience of the Junior Certificate are now expected to develop the ability to comprehend and compose across a more differentiated range of literacies which find expression in numerous discourses and genres.

The personal emphasis that was so significant at primary level, and also to a lesser extent at Junior Certificate, is now subsumed and the orientation is very much on developing in students the language skills that they will need for their adult life.

The syllabus categorises language under the following five general headings:

- The Language of Information

- The Language of Persuasion

- The Language of Argument

- The Language of Narrative

- The Aesthetic use of Language

Within each of these general categories the student is required to study in detail a series of genres, developing an understanding of how they work to create their meanings, how language is shaped and selected to make meanings, and also developing the ability to compose in these genres. This entails a detailed study not alone of what texts are saying but how they are saying it in relation to two domains of Language Awareness, viz., Macro-Language awareness, and Micro-Language awareness.

Since language genres can be described as 'socially and culturally approved forms of language for achieving definite ends', then each genre will have a definite social context and specific linguistic attributes. Macro-language awareness means understanding how the social context shapes the text under such headings as:

- audience

- speaker/writer

- purpose
- tone
- register

Micro-language awareness means understanding how

- words
- syntax
- grammatical structures
- sentences
- paragraphs

are selected and shaped to achieve the specific communicative purposes of the genre.

For example, if a student was looking at the following text he/she would be expected to recognise that it is a fable (a moral tale, unknown author, composed for a public, unknown audience) whose language is spare, active, dramatic, and colloquial so that it can communicate powerfully its moral lesson.

The Muddy Road

Two monks, Tanzan and Ekido, were on a journey back to their monastery. They came to a muddy road. A beautiful woman stood by the side of the road afraid to cross lest her long robe might get destroyed. Tanzan asked, 'May I help you to cross?' The woman gladly agreed. Tanzan took her in his arms and carried her across the road. The monks continued on their journey.

As they neared their monastery Ekido said to Tanzan, 'You know that it is against the rules of our order to even look at a woman. But you have taken a woman in your arms, felt her body against yours and smelled her perfume. It is my duty to report you to the abbot.' Tanzan replied, 'Ekido, my friend, I left the woman behind me at the side of the road, she is obviously still with you'.

The other new perspective introduced at Leaving Certificate is that of critical literacy. This emphasises that all texts are discourses, embedded in specific cultural practices and participating in ways of structuring society in terms of power and significance. All texts seek to position the reader into a way of seeing the world, or, as Aristotle commented, all texts are suasive. Critical literacy helps students to resist, in Freirean terms, the 'suasiveness' of a text, to reflect on its discourse and analyse its implicit values. Perhaps an example will illustrate the point most clearly.

I was in church recently and noticed the following inscription under a statue erected to commemorate a couple who had died some time ago:

In Memory of Daniel and Mrs Harrington

This is a text on which some interesting work could be done on the layout, use of titles and proper names to indicate value systems and assumptions. For example:

- It communicates effectively. Although it is not formally a complete sentence . . . it is a declarative, rhetorical phrase.

- Its choice of words is most interesting: one a personal name – Daniel, the other a formal, functional surname in which the person (who happens to be a woman) is embedded. Who was this woman? Did she have a personal name? Was her personal significance circumscribed only by the fact that she was Daniel Harrington's wife (his Mrs!).

- Again the syntax is worth noting: the order of word precedence clearly reflects a social precedence.

This approach to developing critical literacy comes from the work of Gunther Kress who suggests that every text can be usefully interrogated by asking three simple questions of it:

- Why is this topic being written about?
- How is the topic being written about?
- What other ways of writing about the topic are there? (Kress, 1994: 7)

As can be seen from this simple illustration, true to the philosophy informing this syllabus, the study and development of language and literacies is real, bound into the reading and writing of texts which have a significance for the student either now or in the future.

These approaches to literacy and language development have been influenced by the work of Ronald Carter and the LINC materials produced by the Department of English in Nottingham University (see Carter, 1989). Of significance as well was the research of Gunther Kress on genre theory for developing literacy skills.

In terms of assessment, it is intended that each examination paper in the terminal written examination will focus in such a way that students will have to demonstrate their ability to comprehend some of these genres and also to write effectively in at least one or two of them. In the light of the increased emphasis put on the study of literacy and language, the marks awarded for the language paper will be equivalent to the number of marks awarded for the literature paper. Furthermore it is planned that in the Leaving Certificate examination a certain percentage of marks will be allocated for correctness and appropriateness in the traditional basic skills of spelling and punctuation in order to reinforce society's concern about these matters.

Summary

It should now be clear that throughout the curriculum in English there is a coherence and a sense of development present relative to the nurturing of literacies.

In primary education, the broad foundation of the generic skills of speaking, listening, reading and writing is laid down: the emphasis is on giving the child a sense of competence and confidence in relation to language and making available a rich integrated programme of growth and development.

Then at secondary level, while maintaining the centrality of developing the student's confidence, a gradual change of emphasis becomes evident. The explicit differentiation into a range of generic literacies which takes place at Junior Certificate, points to the increasing stress on students learning the language skills needed to enter society. Finally, at Leaving Certificate, the study of a range of genres emphasises that it is vital for all students to be flexible and adept in their language use, and equally aware of how it is used about them, so that they may in a position to take on their role as adult citizens, competent and confident in being in control of all the literacies they need.

Figure 1 is a speculative attempt to place the three syllabi in English in some kind of position relative to one another and to the assumptions that underpin them. The vertical axis is the axis of Language with poles of Fluency and Accuracy; the horizontal axis is the Human axis of syllabus orientation with its poles of person (child-centred education) and society (genre/subject/discourse-centred education). It needs to be reiterated that this is a speculative diagram: its placing of the syllabi in these relative positions may not be felt by others to be an accurate assessment of their emphasis and orientation.

Figure 1. Polarities in Primary and Secondary English Syllabi

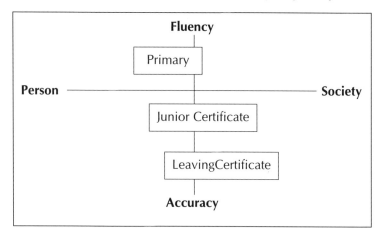

In conclusion I would like to quote from the new Leaving Certificate syllabus a few paragraphs which express the vision of language and literacy informing these syllabi.

> It is a complex task to become literate in modern society. A bewildering range of linguistic forms and styles challenges students . . . Developing control and power over language is the most essential educational achievement for students if they are to become confident, thoughtful and discriminating adults and citizens.
>
> Through using language accurately and appropriately, they themselves can realise a sense of personal significance and discover how words can work for them in revealing meanings, inviting thought and facilitating effective communication. (Department of Education/NCCA, 1997: 5)

These are the educational aims to which all these syllabi aspire: now we can only hope that such worthwhile aspirations are not frustrated by other considerations and agendas, and that appropriate in-career development for teachers will be provided to ensure that they are in a position to bring the promise of these documents to fruition in the classroom.

References

Britton, J. (1972) *Language and Learning*, London: Penguin.

Carter, R. (1989) *LINC (Language in the National Curriculum: materials for professional development)* Nottingham: University of Nottingham Department of English.

Department of Education /NCCA (1990) Junior Certificate English Syllabus, Dublin: NCCA.

Department of Education/NCCA (1997) Leaving Certificate English Syllabus, Dublin: NCCA.

Kress, G. (1994) *Linguistic Processes in Sociocultural Practice*, Victoria: Deakin University Press.

Swift, J. (1712) 'A Proposal For Correcting, Improving and Ascertaining The English Language.' Quoted in: Crowley, T. (1991) *Proper English*, London: Routledge.

12

Assessment in English – principles and practices
Pat Coffey

This paper outlines the guiding principles underpinning assessment in English at second level, indicates briefly some elements of English assessment operative in the classroom, and comments on some general issues relating to the nature of state examinations. It specifically refers to the qualities and characteristics of state examinations especially as they apply to the examining of English and, finally, indicates some recent developments in the examining of English which could have a wider impact in the future. In this regard it draws particular attention to some key developments in the assessment of the English and Communication course in the Leaving Certificate Applied programme where we have witnessed the introduction of some innovative modes of assessment.

Guiding principles

Underpinning the work of the Department of Education and Science in assessment are the five guiding principles of *Charting our Education Future – White Paper on Education*. These are as follows:

- Pluralism
- Equality
- Partnership
- Quality
- Accountability

These principles are equally applicable, of course, in other areas of education, but applying them specifically to assessment and in particular to the assessment of English we can state the following:

Pluralism: Pluralism recognises that individuals differ in the way they learn and that policy formulation in education should value and promote all dimensions of human development. This recognition of difference and individuality would suggest that assessment should be multifaceted in its approach, developing modes and elements which go beyond the traditional and tried, and are congruent with the requirements of the broad range of syllabi being taught in the classroom. We certainly see evidence of a willingness to do just this in the more innovative programmes such as the Leaving Certificate Applied and the Junior Certificate Elementary Programme.

Equality: This principle stresses that the education system should embody a philosophy which embraces all students on a basis of equality. A sustaining philosophy in this regard would seek to promote equality of access, participation and benefit. For this to occur, innovative modes of assessment will have to be developed which will facilitate and enhance equality of treatment and outcome. Given that English is so central in the lives of people, the teaching and assessment of English will have a special role to play in promoting equality and, hopefully, in ameliorating the more detrimental and obvious effects of disadvantage.

Partnership: Effective partnership involves active cooperation in all areas of education between all those with an interest in the education process. Assessment too should be conducted in partnership. In this regard there should be a development of involvement by the partners, including teachers, students, parents, and other groups with a special interest in education, in aspects of the assessment process. Partnership in state examinations can already be seen when subject associations, such as the ATE

(Association of Teachers of English), and the various subject committees of the teachers' unions comment on the examination papers prior to the devising of the marking schemes for assessment. Such comments are taken into consideration when the marking schemes are being devised collegially by the relevant subject advisory teams. Partnership is also put into practice when the final reports of examiners relating to all aspects of the examination paper and the assessment process are taken into account for future reference.

Partnership also requires transparency so that the partners are given opportunity to understand the assessment process itself and to exercise their rights and responsibilities in relation to it. *The Information Folder – Leaving Certificate Higher Level English, 1997*, which was issued to schools in the first week of January, could be regarded as an example of such transparency. This folder contained the marking scheme for the 1997 paper, exemplars of standard, the Chief Examiner's Final Report, and the Chief Examiner's Report to the Minister on the Appeal Process in English. The latter report recommended strongly that information regarding the standards obtaining at Leaving Certificate – Higher Level English, the examination techniques appropriate to the level, and the detail of arrangements and processes for examining should be widely disseminated throughout the community of teachers of English.

Quality: The principle of quality enjoins that the state should ensure and promote the highest standard of education and learning for all. It entails a variety of interdependent factors including the quality of the curriculum, teaching and assessment. Indeed, assessment can and must be described in terms of its quality. The Department, for its part, constantly reviews its systems ensuring that the highest quality of assessment is in place and that the rigour required to ensure quality is comprehensively and even-handedly applied. The establishment by the Minister of an expert advisory group charged with providing independent advice and evaluation on the operation of state certificate examinations is noteworthy in this regard. Relating specifically to the assessment of English, one of the recommendations of the Report on the Appeal Process in English was that the arrangements and procedures for assessment should be reviewed further as part of the Department's own evaluation of procedures for all aspects of examinations.

Accountability: Because education occupies so central a position in individual and social development, appropriate processes must be operated at various levels to evaluate the effectiveness of education policy, provision and outcomes. Assessment processes cannot be excluded from such evaluation. Assessment cannot operate in some sort of ivory tower. At all levels within the system, but especially at state level, assessment is required to be accountable.

Assessment, of course, is also important as part of the evaluative process of the entire system of education, providing useful data to the national authorities relating to the effectiveness and efficiency of the system and its component parts. In this regard assessment is itself an instrument of both quality and accountability.

Assessment in the classroom

It is absolutely essential to stress that assessment goes far beyond what happens in state examinations. Indeed, careful assessment in the classroom underpins all good educational practice and supports curricular objectives. The skills and procedures of assessment are fundamental to the teacher's work and vital to the learner's progress. Assessment is usually concerned with the gathering of information related to student's knowledge, under-standing, skills and aptitudes, and encompasses all the methods used to evaluate the achievements of individuals and groups. It evaluates the full range of abilities and provides information which is reported to parents and students alike regarding progress and difficulties.

With regard to English specifically, there are many forms of assessment in operation in the classroom. These include summative assessment where what has been achieved in the course of a year, a term, a unit or a module is formally assessed by the teacher, frequently through written examination. Assessment can also be informal and continuous in nature, encompassing occasional tests, written answers to questions on topics, oral ques-tioning and many other forms. Such assessment has a formative function, contributing to the ongoing development of the student. Essay writing also forms a necessary part of English assessment. Writing practice is necessary for all students of English and careful and positive feedback to students allows opportunities for improvement and development. Teachers of English also allow students to participate in assessment in a partnership mode when students, under teacher guidance, actively engage in the editing, honing and crafting of their own written work as encouraged by *Junior Certificate English – Guidelines for Teachers* (a form of self-assessment), and also when students comment upon and edit the work of their classmates (a form of peer-assessment).

Observation of students' work in class is a constant feature of teachers' work and results in assessment judgements on a continuous basis. This form of assessment fulfils a number of key functions.

- It allows the teacher to monitor the rate of class progress or the individual student's development.

- It provides the teacher with the means of identifying the needs of individual students.

- It allows for the modification of curriculum content, making it more suitable to the needs of the students. This is particularly appropriate in Junior Cycle English where the open, unprescribed nature of the course allows for change of direction by the teacher when required.

- It allows for the modification of teacher strategies which will facilitate effective learning.

Teacher observation, therefore, is an essential component of the cyclic process of classroom activity which encompasses teaching, learning, assessing, identifying individual and group needs, evaluating teaching strategies and planning future learning experiences.

Whichever form assessment takes – formative or summative – it is important that assessment procedures be comprehensive enough to test the full range of abilities across the curriculum and to evaluate all the elements of learning. It is equally important that assessment methods support the entire range of curricular objectives.

State examinations

State examinations are formal, summative and external to the school. They are important for purposes of certification and progression and, in this regard, have an extraordinary currency and acceptability among the community at large. However, it is essential to remember that they form merely a part of the entire assessment picture. What has been described above in relation to classroom-based assessment is equally important and, consequently, we should not allow state examinations to exercise an undue dominance over the entire enterprise of teaching and learning. Neither can state examinations be ignored. It is important, therefore, to look more closely at the specific assessment principles which underpin their current form and any shape they may take in the future.

Qualities of state examinations

I would now like to examine the qualities which state examinations endeavour to espouse, with particular reference to how these qualities operate in English. For state examinations to be meaningful they should display a number of key qualities. These are as follows:

- Fitness for purpose
- Validity
- Differentiation
- Reliability
- Standardisation

Fitness for purpose

In the devising of examinations a number of important questions should be considered so that the examinations which are offered are, in the first instance, suitable and appropriate. These questions include the following:

Why are these questions being asked?

What aspects of learning are we examining in asking them?

Who should be involved in conducting the assessment?

How should assessment be executed – by written, oral, or aural examination?

In summary, the Fitness for Purpose principle requires us, on the one hand, to be absolutely clear as to why we are assessing and, on the other hand, to find the most appropriate techniques or styles of examining to fulfil that purpose. Assessment, it must be stressed, is a creative process that can be as varied and interesting as teaching and learning.

Validity

For questions to be valid in an examination they should be central to what students are asked to learn. Questions should not be asked which are from outside the syllabus. Neither should there be peripheral or trick questions. Only questions stemming from explicit syllabus content give the paper its content validity. An invalid assessment is one where the context or structure or requirements of the assessment task actually get in the way and prevent a candidate from showing the reality of what she or he knows, understands and can do.

The way assessment is presented is also part of assessment validity. In presenting an examination paper, for example, the aim should be to allow each candidate the best opportunity to show what you are actually looking for. This, when successfully achieved, gives the paper presentation validity.

Examination papers as far as possible should be inviting and accessible to the candidates. The use of colour, graphics and pictorial illustrations, such as are in use at Junior Certificate English, are most helpful in this regard. Other factors which come into play are the following:

- Clarity, i.e. clear layout, clear rubrics and instructions
- Readability, i.e. the correct level of difficulty in terms of reading level
- Legibility, i.e. the use of appropriate typeface, font, print size etc.
- Appropriate timing, i.e. sufficient time per question, or in sections with a number of parts ensuring that the entire section is doable
- Appropriate length, i.e. ensuring that passages given as stimuli are appropriate in length and contain sufficient matter to give rise to interesting and challenging questions
- Relevance to the topic being examined, to the syllabus, and to the candidates' experience

With the best of intentions it may not always be possible to get it absolutely and totally right. Individual candidates are different and it may be extremely difficult to account fully for each one of them. If certain difficulties are known to have arisen in the course of examinations, however, every effort should be made at marking conferences to rectify the problem, ensuring that the good of the candidate is kept to the fore at all times.

Differentiation

Differentiation in assessment is about constructing assessment mechanisms that allow all candidates the opportunity to demonstrate what they can do. It also offers those assessing the opportunity of discriminating between differences in attainment. This is achieved in a number of ways.

In the first instance, it is achieved by differentiation in level, that is, by offering papers for assessment pitched at different levels of ability. In Junior Certificate English, for instance, though the syllabus indicated that assessment would be offered at two levels – Ordinary Level and Higher Level, it is, in fact, offered at three levels – Ordinary, Higher and Foundation. The introduction of the third level, Foundation, was particularly important as this level caters for a particularly important clientele many of whom receive remedial assistance in schools. Candidates who would find it difficult to cope at either of the other two levels are now achieving success at this level.

A particular difficulty which arises from the provision of three levels is that of knowing which level is the most appropriate for a given candidate. It is clear from examiners' reports over the past number of years that some candidates would have been better served if they had taken the examination at a different level, either above or below the level at which they did in fact sit. However, this is a difficulty which can be overcome in the light of the developing experience of individual teachers who advise candidates in these matters and also by the publication of marking schemes and Chief Examiner's reports which provide information regarding standards pertaining at each of the levels.

Differentiation by outcome is also operative in examinations in English. By this is meant that the same assessment test offered to a large cohort of candidates within a level is constructed in such a way that it allows those at the top end of the ability range of the particular cohort to perform to the best of their ability while allowing those at the bottom of the ability range of the cohort to do well also. A high failure rate at a particular level may indicate that a significant number of candidates entered at the incorrect level.

Finally, we have differentiation within task. This occurs when a task or section or question which has a number of sub-parts is arranged in such a way that the constituent parts are organised in ascending order of difficulty. This provides for an initial invitation into the task to all participating candidates but also allows for the testing of progressively higher order and more difficult skills as candidates work their way through the task. An analogous image here is the chart in the optician's examining room which presents more easily discerned lettering at the top and then becomes progressively more difficult for patients as they move down the chart. English papers, particularly at Junior Certificate, have something of this incremental approach built into their various sections. However, in devising tasks incorporating this particular approach one has to be careful that the more difficult tasks at the end are not beyond the reach of the general run of candidates taking the level. Rather these more demanding tasks should allow for a variety of response, according to individual ability. This varying level of response is what allows for differentiation or discrimination in the marking and for the 'scatter' of grades awarded.

Reliability

Assessment is a human process. As such, it is subject to all the possible variables that this entails. The pursuit of reliability, therefore, involves, on the one hand, a recognition of the possible variables, human or otherwise, that could affect the outcome of assessment and, on the other hand, the establishment of procedures designed to remove or reduce, as far as possible, the effects of these same variables. Among the variables that could impact on reliability are the following:

(*a*) Variations in the interpretation of the criteria for assessment

(*b*) The perception of the individual examiner

(*c*) The circumstances and environment in which assessment takes place

(*d*) The nature of the examination and specifically the nature of the questions being asked

(*a*) It is essential that there be clarity of understanding by each examiner regarding the agreed marking scheme. Differing interpretations of criteria are a major variable. Hence the importance of a comprehensive and clear marking scheme. Emphasis must also be placed on the training of assistant examiners at conference prior to the commencement of marking. There must be clearly defined roles for the Chief Examiner and advising examiners who monitor the ongoing work of assistant examiners. Provision must also be made for revision of work when it is found that an individual examiner has strayed from the criteria for assessment, wholly or in part. Details as to how all of the above operates in relation to English were included in the Information Folder – Leaving Certificate Higher Level English, 1997 which was issued to schools.

(*b*) Regarding the perception of the individual examiner, while it is clear that examiners bring a wealth of teaching and assessment experience to the task of examining, it has to be stressed to all involved in this task that purely personal standards of judgement are not to be applied. These are replaced by standards and criteria which are agreed upon at the marking conferences held prior to examining, honed in careful training, and applied not only in the original marking but also in the appeal process which follows.

The perception of the individual examiner may also be problematic in the area of oral examinations. Indeed, in oral examinations there is the added difficulty of examiners interacting differently with candidates face to face. This adds a new interpersonal dynamic to the assessment situation, a dynamic which is of necessity variable and consequently more difficult to control. In the oral examination for English and Communication in the Leaving Certificate Applied programme, conducted for the first time in 1997, it was stressed to examiners that a sameness of questioning and a sameness of interview approach should be applied in the examining of all candidates. There is no doubting that the different personalities of examiners can introduce variation in candidate response and performance. As far as is possible these differences must be minimised in training prior to assessment.

(*c*) Examinations must take place under the same conditions for all and be invigilated in the same manner. The Department is extremely careful about this and issues a comprehensive set of instructions to all superintendents of certificate examinations every year. It is also required that examination centres fulfil certain criteria regarding suitability. These centres are monitored by the Department's inspectorate in the course of the examinations.

(*d*) The reliability of an examination may be affected by the nature of the examination itself. Objective tests with each item having one right answer are most likely to satisfy reliability. However, the testing of single objective items is not what generally occurs in the assessment of English in state examinations. Nor, given the requirements of the syllabi at both junior and senior cycles, would such an approach be appropriate or desirable. Questions asked in English examinations, particularly at Leaving Certificate level, require in many instances essay-type answers. These of their nature do not lend themselves to easy assessment.

Perhaps examples would make this point clear. If, for instance, the following question is asked – 'What is the name of King Lear's kind daughter?' – it is obvious that the answers given by candidates will be either right or wrong. Because of the objective nature of the information being elicited, the assessment of the answer to the question will be absolutely reliable. However, it may not always be appropriate to ask such questions. It may, indeed, be appropriate to ask such questions on some of the Junior Certificate examination papers, particularly at points where simple comprehension is being tested. It would be totally inappropriate, however, on either of the Leaving Certificate examination papers.

If, on the other hand, a question is asked based on the statement 'Our initial disapproval of Lear in Shakespeare's King Lear develops ultimately into a profound sympathy for him' (Leaving Certificate – Higher Level 1997), it is clear, given the requirements of the syllabus and the course, that the question is wholly appropriate and valid. However, because the answer does not have objective certainty and will, accordingly, vary from candidate to candidate in terms of content, approach, manner in which it is written, etc., it cannot be assessed with the same level of reliability as the first question.

This is not to say that assessment of the second more discursive question is unreliable. What it does point up, however, is the necessity for an approach to assessment which is more complex and sophisticated in its nature. Such an approach will involve a form of assessment which takes into account criteria such as the following:

- the accuracy of the information given by the candidate
- the relevance of the information given to the question being asked
- the coherence of the argument put forward by the candidate
- the plausibility of the answer
- the appropriateness of the language in which the answer is couched

These are extremely complex assessment judgements and require experience and training on the part of those involved in the examining. Such training, in the case of English, involves the examination of pre-selected samples in the light of an agreed marking scheme and the honing and sharpening of an informed judgement which can compare one answer to a particular question against another answer to the same question. After all, the examination at this level is, by and large, norm referenced, that is, the work of each candidate is compared against some particular standard regarded as the norm.

A similar approach is required in relation to essay writing in the examination. Here the criteria for assessment are very specific, indeed, involving judgements on the ideas of the essay, the structure of the essay, the candidate's level of expression and the candidate's level of mechanical control of language.

Standardisation

An aspect of the assessment process which is vitally important in state examinations is, of course, standardisation. This refers to the procedures in operation which ensure that the same standard of informed judgement is applied to the answers of each candidate in a particular examination.

In English there are a number of procedures in place to ensure this. These include the following:

- the devising of the marking scheme – a task undertaken collegially by the Chief Examiner, the Chief Advising Examiner and the entire advisory team;
- the use of photocopied samples of candidates' work in the examination in order to pre-test the marking scheme and

to establish a standard – exemplars are published by the Department from time to time;

- briefing the entire team of assistant examiners in order to ensure understanding of and familiarity with the procedures for examining, the marking scheme, the standard being applied and key instructions;

- the assigning of each assistant examiner to an advising examiner who monitors and advises according to set procedures for the duration of the marking;

- the monitoring of scripts by advising examiners in the course of the marking;

- the revising of scripts by assistant examiners if required to do so by their advisers.

Examiners are also issued with certain key instructions with regard to how they should proceed in the course of the marking. These include the following:

- To expect a wide variation of standard in the scripts allocated to them. Each script is to be treated individually. If an examiner encounters a sequence of particular grades she/he should realise that such a phenomenon is a possibility.

- Not to penalise for irrelevance in essays without first consulting with the advising examiner.

- To code candidates' answers when points relevant to given questions are made. Such codes usually consist of the first letter of a key term in a question e.g. 'D' for disapproval of King Lear and 'S' for sympathy for King Lear (cf. Marking Scheme – 1997).

- To underline all errors encountered on candidates' scripts.

- To comment in writing on the scripts, on both the positive and negative aspects of the material under examination. Such comments assist examiners in deciding on a final mark for answers.

- To review scripts where final mark totals fall just short of a grade threshold. Scripts, for example, where the final total is two per cent or less short of a grade are reviewed with the purpose of determining whether or not they merit the higher grade in the light of the set standard. Such a review does not guarantee an automatic increase in marks.

These then are some of the procedures and instructions in place for ensuring that the agreed standard is applied to each candidate individually. All of these procedures are constantly reviewed in order to increase rigour in standardisation

Developments in assessment in English

The current Leaving Certificate syllabus has been examined for well over twenty years. The Junior Certificate syllabus was first examined in 1992. Both have been examined by written terminal examination only. However, there has in recent times been a number of significant developments in the assessment of English in state examinations. Much of this development has occurred in the English and Communication course of the Leaving Certificate Applied programme. This course is fundamentally different to anything put in place for English in the past. While space does not allow for an in-depth examination here of its content and its teaching methodologies, suffice it to say that the course displays a very strong emphasis on the more functional skills of English, both oral and written, as they have practical application in the environment of work and enterprise.

The course consist of four modules as follows:

• Communications and the Working World
• The Communications Media
• Communications and Enterprise
• Critical Literacy and Composition

Each of these four modules is valued at one credit out of a possible hundred credits for the entire programme, and these four credits for English and Communication can be achieved provided certain key assignments related to each of the modules are completed and there is ninety per cent attendance by the student for the module.

The oral skills of students are assessed at various points in the programme and not just as outcomes of the English and Communication course. In the two years of the programme, students are assessed in nine major student tasks which they complete in various elements of the programme. As part of the assessment the students present these nine tasks to external

examiners appointed by the Department of Education and
Science and are interviewed individually. What is significant
here, from the perspective of English, is that oral as well as
written proficiencies of candidates form part of the assessment in
each task. This stress on oral proficiency in particular has had an
important influence on the emphasis given in the classroom to
the development of students' oral skills.

Even more important, however, in this regard, has been the
introduction of the first oral examination in English at any level
of state examinations. This oral examination, accounting for a
third of the marks in the final examination for English and
Communication, was conducted in June 1997 when Leaving
Certificate Applied students were assessed by external examiners
appointed by the Department.

Yet another innovation in the final examination of the English
and Communication course was the introduction of an audio-
visual component. In this component candidates were shown an
audio-visual presentation consisting of a sequence from a television drama and asked to write answers to a number of questions
based on the sequence. Candidates found this approach highly
stimulating and responded very well to it. It must be obvious
that such a component of assessment has enormous possibilities
for the assessment of many other aspects of English. Drama, Film
Studies and Media Studies are just some of the areas which
come readily to mind in this regard.

The English and Communication course in the Leaving
Certificate Applied programme deserves specific mention because
it is here that assessment in English is at its most innovative.
Programmes such as the Leaving Certificate Applied with their
exciting approaches to teaching and learning and their relatively
small cohorts of students do, in fact, afford an opportunity to
push out the boundaries of assessment. However, as often
happens with developing programmes, the innovation which
accompanies them tends to backwash into the more established
mainstream system. This, of course, does not always happen
immediately nor as quickly, perhaps, as many would wish.

In this regard it would be important to indicate that the
Minister for Education and Science, who has a particular interest
in oral communication in English, has requested the NCCA to
investigate the feasibility of introducing an oral examination at

Junior Certificate level. Such an examination, if it were to be introduced, would indeed be a major development in mainstream English assessment – a development which could have profound implications for the teaching of oral skills in the classroom.

References

Department of Education (1990) *The Junior Certificate – English Syllabus*, Dublin: Government Publications

Department of Education and Science (1997) *The Information Folder – Leaving Certificate Higher Level English, 1997*, Dublin: Government Publications.

Department of Education and Science (1997) 'Rules and Programmes for Secondary Schools – 1997/1998.' Mimeo. Dublin: DES.

Department of Education/NCCA (1995) *Leaving Certificate Applied – Programme Materials*, Dublin: NCCA.

Department of Education/NCCA (1995) *Leaving Certificate Applied – English and Communication, Draft Modules*, Dublin: NCCA.

Department of Education/NCCA (1990) *The Junior Certificate – English, Guidelines for Teachers*, Dublin: NCCA.

Government of Ireland (1995) *Charting our Education Future – White Paper on Education*, Dublin: Government Publications.

Part 5

The challenges of non-standard English and learning support

13

Issues in learning support

Ann Whelan

Teaching English to students with learning difficulties poses a particular challenge. Research conducted both in Ireland and abroad would suggest that up to 20 per cent of our students have learning difficulties. These can range from the mild and short term to the severe and long term with many gradations in between. Further complication is added by the fact that students of average intelligence who present with learning difficulties often do not have the skills required to demonstrate their abilities. Dysgraphic students, for example, have difficulties in writing and in their cases another medium must be explored through which the student may present evidence of knowledge. Taken all in all, then, the issue of learning support is both timely and appropriate for inclusion in any discussion of the teaching and usage of English in this country.

The main purpose of this chapter is to outline and explore briefly the characteristics of certain of the more common conditions requiring learning support in our classroom. It is hoped that this may help dispel some of the misunderstandings and myths that can surround practice and possibilities in the learning support area. These conditions are: dyslexia, attention deficit/hyperactivity disorder (AD/HD), Autistic Spectrum Disorder, Asperger's Syndrome, dyspraxia, and acquired memory disorders.

Dyslexia

Of those 20 per cent of students who suffer from a specific learning disorder the great majority will be dyslexic. Dyslexia is an umbrella term that covers a multitude of reading difficulties. More than 40 definitions have been offered to describe the condition. Essentially, the disorder presents as an unexpected difficulty in learning to read. The unexpectedness occurs because the student, of otherwise average intelligence, should make age-appropriate gains in acquiring literacy skills but does not do so. Dyslexic students do in time learn how to read but reading will always be much more difficult and less fluent for them than it is for their peers.

While the term 'dyslexia' originally meant *word blindness*, much more is now known about the condition. For example, it is now known that working memory is restricted or limited in some students. What is restricted is the ability to hold in memory simultaneously all of the elements of a task that is either sequenced, as in reading or learning multiplication tables, or anything that requires many simultaneous operations. There is more to reading fluently than meets the eye and an adequate working memory is based on skill required for the task. Working memory comprises both short-term visual memory and short term auditory memory. These two memories are relatively easy to test and testing them will usually form part of any assessment of dyslexia.

Sight/sound correspondence, that is, the ability to sound the letter, to say its name when its shape is recognised, is one of the building bricks of learning to read. Some dyslexic students never become 'builders'. From an early age they continue to have difficulty with the phonic aspect of reading. They may learn the sight-sound correspondences, and may sound out letters and letter combinations but they will continue to experience difficulties in synthesising or in putting these combinations together. An example of this is a child who masters three-letter words such as *car* and *pet*. It may seem a fairly straightforward task to combine these into *carpet*. However, such combinations elude the dyslexic student.

Research into the effect of cross laterality, that is, of a situation where students favour their right hands and feet but have dominant left eyes, has increased our knowledge of the condition. Students who are cross lateral have been found, in 90 per cent of cases, to have difficulties with short-term visual memory. While this has implications for the acquisition of reading it also causes more wide-ranging problems. The most serious of these is a difficulty with transcribing from the board. Instead of being able to memorise quickly a few words or items at a time from the board, affected students must continue to raise the head each time to look at each word or item. They have an inability to memorise words in combination. As with all learning disorders, the earlier the diagnosis, and the speedier the intervention, the more the student will benefit.

Language processing disorders are also included under the dyslexic umbrella. The language disordered child may be inclined to say 'crips' for 'crisps', 'piscetti' for 'spaghetti', 'hopsickel' for 'hospital', and so on, and will utter many malapropisms. In Dublin parlance the 'things-on-the-yokes' brigade may have an underlying and undiagnosed language processing disorder. There is frequently a lag in the oral vocabulary acquisition of these students. Not only is their vocabulary more restricted but they have been observed by parents and classroom teachers deliberately to seek out the companionship of younger students with whom they would communicate more easily. Parents often note that these students acquire language skills later than their siblings do. Most youngsters begin to talk in sentences by the age of two to two-and-a-half years. It has been noted for language-disordered youngsters that the onset of language does not begin until later – until the age of three or maybe four.

Language processing disorders may need intervention from speech therapists. In some parts of the country a happy union of teachers and remedial linguists has already taken place. The linguist sees the child, works out a system of exercises to improve language skills, and passes some of these exercises on to the teacher. The teacher then practises daily with the affected child. While this situation is in place, it is not yet widespread.

There is a school of thought that rejects the label of dyslexia. Instead, practitioners in this school would prefer to use the term of 'specific reading disorder'. This argument is not new. It has been about for a number of years. It is true that a cluster of problems can lead to a specific reading disorder, but this is not really what is important. What is important is that the language disordered student, who is offered the assistance of remedial linguistics, will show an improvement in speech/language and this improvement usually has the effect of enhancing the student's reading skills.

Attention Deficit (Hyperactivity) Disorder

The second most frequently seen learning disorder is Attention Deficit (Hyperactivity) Disorder. This disorder has one foot in each of two camps – educational and medical/neurological. At the moment, in Ireland, one foot is leaning more heavily in the medical camp as Our Lady's Hospital for Sick Children, Crumlin, is in the process of setting up an AD/HD clinic. This clinic hopes to address matters of relevance to students and to their parents. Referral is through paediatric neurologists in the hospital.

The attention-disordered student in the classroom can be difficult to teach. By definition the student is restless, fidgety, frequently out of seat, oppositional, and talks excessively. Two methods of managing the disorder are suggested: teachers and parents are encouraged to provide a structured environment, advance knowledge of timetables, consistency of response, lists as memory aids and behaviour modification strategies. The second method of management is chemical management most frequently by amphetamine based drugs. Some parents are understandably reluctant to impose a drug regime on their children while others will cite the strong benefits to be obtained. A drug regime may produce as many as seventeen side effects from which some students suffer.

In 50 per cent of cases of AD/HD, particularly in adolescence, the disorder has been found to be comorbid with other learning disorders. There is also a history of comorbidity with depression. The chemical containment route is frequently reassessed in teenagers for this reason. If comorbid with depression, should a second drug, such as an anti-depressant, be introduced and what will be the long and short-term psychological sequelae? When a chemical management programme is offered, parents are usually advised to monitor any side effects and to report back to the prescribing psychiatrist or neurologist on such effects. At second level, attention-disordered boys, who outnumber their female peers by a ratio of 5:1, must also deal with hormonal changes brought about by adolescence. The combination can be an unfortunate one and some disordered students are asked to leave the school usually because of disruptive behaviour. At the moment out-of-school students are offered one-to-one tuition by the Department of Education for a number of hours each week. Grateful parents, while grasping at this straw, consider that this is not the most satisfactory compromise. Some schools have put place in classroom assistants or have made a supervised quiet room available to attention disordered students where they can spend some 'time out' and from there return to the classroom.

Autistic Spectrum Disorder

Autistic spectrum disorder covers learning disorders from classic autism to Asperger's Syndrome. Classic autism is defined as a condition in which reciprocal social interaction is gross and not sustained. There may be marked impairment in the use of multiple non-verbal behaviours, for example, eye-to-eye contact, body postures and gestures. A marked failure to develop good peer relationships is also noted. Individuals may also be oblivious to other children including siblings and may have no concept of the needs of others. Classic autism is so debilitating that it is usually diagnosed early, by three years, and diagnosed children are usually referred for specialist teaching in specialist schools.

Experts usually consider Asperger's Syndrome to be on a continuum with autism, in which children exhibit similar but milder social impairments. It is usually diagnosed much later because symptoms do not stand out in the same way. While the Syndrome was formerly thought to be relatively rare, new research conducted in Sweden put the incidence at about one in 300. If there is a similar prevalence in Ireland it is likely that most medium to large schools will have at least one enrolled student with the Syndrome.

Disorders such as this come into the category of hidden disabilities. The disability usually does not have any outward easily identifiable characteristics. Many affected students walk with an unusual gait, but so do students who are unaffected.

In Asperger's Syndrome, Tony Atwood (1998) outlines six pathways to diagnosis. The first one is monitoring a student previously diagnosed as being autistic. Because these students are monitored regularly, it has been found that with early intervention and therapy some children thrive in primary schools and may later be re-diagnosed. Students with speech/language difficulties, having been referred for speech therapy, who do not make expected social gains, may also be reclassified as being on this spectrum. The diagnosis of a relative with Asperger's Syndrome may also point the diagnostician in the direction as there tends to be a genetic component to the Syndrome. Students in primary schools who cope reasonably well but who are loners or may have eccentric tendencies do not do as well at second-level school. Here the onset of adolescence combined with the lack of social acceptance can cause the student to become depressed, and on a referral for depression one of the underlying causes may turn out to be Asperger's Syndrome.

Because symptoms such as difficulty in communicating with others may be symptomatic of more than one disorder, early referral for assessment is recommended. Early intervention such as social skills training, Circle Time, role play and role modelling can all advance the social skills of affected students. Early intensive intervention for both teachers and parents is currently the subject of ongoing research.

Dyspraxia

Praxis is the ability to use hands and feet in a coordinated way. The dyspraxic student may not be able to acquire motor skills in the same way as her or his peers. Dyspraxia is sometimes called the clumsy child syndrome. It is possible to identify the syndrome early in the child's life. Affected children in the first year of life cry frequently. They do not reach motor developmental stages at age appropriate dates; for example, they may never go through the stage of crawling. Parents state that these children were 'bottom shufflers', that is, they shuffled along rather than crept on all fours.

Not being able to use limbs appropriately is one of the first recognisable symptoms. For the school-age child, difficulties in motor control become more obvious. The child may experience great difficulty in holding a pencil or a crayon. Feeding problems are also noted. These include an awkwardness in holding cutlery, in self-feeding and in drinking. Not only does the dyspraxic child find it difficult to drink from a glass but she or he may send the glass flying across the table in an attempt to pick it up. Dressing, taking clothes off and putting them on can sometimes present insurmountable problems for the younger child.

When assessed on standardised tests these students show a profile of a cluster of depressed scores for certain sub tests particularly those involving visuo-motor skills. This profile can point the diagnostician in the direction of dyspraxia. Typically too, the affected student is able to count, add and subtract but cannot move on to the next stage which involves writing down answers obtained in these tasks. Students tend to be clumsy in the playground, bumping into others. In oral dyspraxia the speech may be affected when the student experiences some dysfluency and has difficulty in communicating clearly with peers. What may seem like an inability to make friends, is found when analysed, for these students to have more to do with clumsiness in so many areas that potential friends may not have the required patience for a sustained friendship.

Following diagnosis, a multi-pronged approach is indicated for maximum effect. Occupational therapists trained to understand the condition provide the best advice for parents. These therapists provide training in fine motor skills required for such tasks as writing, cutting with scissors, threading and tying shoe laces. If parents become members of the treatment team they can help by seeing that exercises are carried out daily. Research indicates that an improvement is noted following treatment. It is also recommended that progress be monitored on a regular basis: a twice-yearly evaluation is usually advised.

Acquired memory disorders

Each year a number of school-aged children are involved in accidents. Research conducted in Ireland and elsewhere suggests that those with most severe consequences are road traffic accidents. The pattern of male dominance prevails here as with other learning disorders: boys outnumber girls by a ratio of 2:1. Where the accident has involved traumatic head and/or brain injury, the length of the coma, the length of hospitalisation and results of a CT scan can all help to give an indication of the damage caused. Research generally indicates that there are physical and psychological sequelae following on CHI (closed head injury).

Because each head injury is different, the effects too will be different. The location of the blow will affect the outcome. If the left hemisphere has been affected, the student's motor performance may show impairment and there are implications for language skills from left hemisphere trauma. Front temporal effects include difficulties with sustaining attention, lack of foresight and planning and disinhibition in speech and actions. Disinhibition of speech can cause the student problems when she or he may use language inappropriately or say the first thing that pops into her or his mind.

Amnesia or memory loss is a core symptom of brain damage. The injured child who has regained consciousness may be unable to remember events leading to the accident. Disorientation and confusion are some noted post traumatic effects. A weakened ability to record new information has also been noted. Such aspects of memory as learning new material, recall and recognition may all be impaired. Recall and recognition affect everyday life in that the student may have difficulty in finding her or his way to school, to the shops or around other locations formerly familiar to her or him.

Furthermore, following on from their injury, students tend to tire more easily. The tiredness can affect concentration on school subjects. They may also find that studying imposes stress. Rest is important and these students may need special management by school authorities. Such management might include a shorter school day. For example, the student might come in for half of the day, take a reduced number of subjects, or a room may be provided where the student might go to rest for a short period. Sensitive and sympathetic handling of the injured student will help on the road to recovery.

Closing comment

What does the future hold for learning support? Recent legislation (Education Act 1998) recognises for the first time the unique position within our education system of students with learning support needs. Consequent future provision is – finally – likely to include an increased number of learning support teachers at both primary and second levels. Schools will avail themselves of the services of these resource teachers by applying for support on behalf of students with documented learning disorders. Schools may also be able to offer reduced class sizes for such students. The exact process of identifying and documenting the learning support needs of individual students is, however, yet unclear. This is an area of extreme importance if we are to provide effective and appropriate learning support within our schools.

English is a core subject in the curriculum and the ability to practise it fluently is an important lifeskill. Success with English is both fundamental and essential to the educational achievement of every student including those with learning difficulties. It is to be hoped that current moves to raise the profile of learning support in schools reflects this importance and will enable students with learning difficulties to achieve levels of literacy appropriate to living in Ireland on the cusp of the twenty-first century.

References

Atwood, T. (1998) *Asperger's Syndrome: A Guide for Parents and Professionals*, London: Jessica Kingsley.

BBC (1997) *Teaching Today: Dyslexia in the Primary Classroom* (BBC Video and Book), London: BBC Publications.

Department for Education and Science UK (1994) *Pupils with Problems*. Mimeograph series, London: HMSO.

Hallowell, E. and J. Ratey (1994) *Driven to Distraction*, New York: Simon & Schuster.

Hanna, D., Smyth, E., McCullagh, J., O'Leary, R. and D. McMahon (1996) *Co-education and Gender Equality*, Dublin: Oak Tree Press.

Hunt, P. (Ed.) (1998) *Praxis Makes Perfect 2*, Hitchin: The Dyspraxia Foundation.

Martin, K. (1997). *Does My Child have a Speech Problem?*, Chicago, IL: Chicago Review Press.

McCormack, W. (1998) *Lost for Words*, Dublin: Tower Press.

Rudel, R. (1988) *Assessment of Developmental Learning Disorders – A Neuropsychological Approach*, New York: Basic Books.

Santostefano, S. (1995) *Integrative Psychotherapy for Children and Adolescents with AD / HD*, New Jersey: Jason Aronson.

Thomson, P. and P. Gilchrist (1996) (eds) *Dyslexia: A Multi Disciplinary Approach*, London: Stanley Thornes.

14

'Big mad words': language variation in schools

Gerry Mac Ruairc

This analysis of language in education is based on the widely held assumption that language is central to the individual, to the group and to society in general (Richardson, 1991). It is through language that we achieve a definition of ourselves and our lives as members of society. Language begins with everyday experience, it controls the way in which we experience, understand and manage our lives. It is a window to our innermost thoughts as individuals. The words we use, and the grammatical patterns that shape and hold them together, come entirely from outside ourselves (Milroy and Milroy, 1991). Our social context teaches us our language and language makes us ourselves. Since language is the chief tool with which we create our personal and social identity it follows that the different meanings developed through language are central to the individual and the social group.

Language stratification in society

In a society characterised by inequality and conflict, all language and meaning systems are not regarded as being of equal value. Many different language varieties exist and each is accorded a social prestige. The way one speaks and how one expresses oneself are established social indicators (Montgomery, 1995).

> Doctors do not sound like dockers anywhere, and building workers do not speak like businessmen . . . if you hear someone say 'I ain't got it yet' or 'I've no got it yet' he is more likely to be a docker than a doctor. (Trudgill, 1983, in Edwards, 1989: 13)

The language variety held by an individual can have a significant impact on success or failure within the education system specifically and within society in general. The most prestigious language variety is often the language variety that is of most social and economic value and is also the variety possessed by the dominant class (Bourdieu, 1991). It is the dominant class which has the power to decide what constitutes prestige linguistic norms. Maintenance of this variety, and the prestige associated with it, becomes the concern of the dominant class and the institutions that uphold its position. The methods and processes used in the control of access to the prestige form of the language play a significant role in the social stratification of language varieties and the resultant marginalisation of certain social groups.

The fact that those groups who are linguistically marginalised are often the same groups who live in impoverished or otherwise disadvantaged areas may be masking the need to deal with linguistic difference in the Irish context. Studies of language difference in an Irish context are rare. Yet Ireland, although reasonably insulated from the impact of different ethnic groups and their associated languages and subcultures, is far from linguistically homogeneous. It is worthwhile noting that 'if a society is stratified, then as language enters into the life of that society . . . it too will display stratification' (Montgomery, 1995: 64).

The link between educational failure and the lower socio-economic classes is widely documented (see, for example, Drudy and Lynch, 1993). Years of research have endeavoured to establish the causes of this failure. Research focusing on the role of language and linguistic differences in explaining educational failure is relatively recent, gaining impetus only after 1965 (see Corson, 1990). Linguistic discontinuity between the home and the school is now considered to be one of the chief factors associated with educational failure (Edwards, 1985; Stubbs, 1983).

Sociolinguistics

Sociolinguistics, as a recent development in the study of language in society, focuses on the study of speech and how language functions in society. Within sociolinguistics there are many firmly held opinions that link language varieties with social stratification. Some language varieties are considered more beautiful than others and some are considered more logical (Milroy and Milroy, 1991; Montgomery, 1995). Wilkinson and Trudgill (1977) proposed a three tier hierarchy for the prestige associated with various English accents. Received Pronunciation (RP) was considered to be the most prestigious, next were British regional accents and last were the accents associated with large urban industrial centres (Trudgill, 1977). These attitudes are all socially constructed since there is no linguistic basis for any such assumptions. Linguistically there is no hierarchy of signs (Burr, 1995). The sign is arbitrary (Saussure, 1974) and this doctrine of the arbitrariness of the sign, so central to linguistics, leads us to the assumption that no language is better or worse than another on linguistic grounds alone (Milroy and Milroy, 1991). Therefore, the considerations of superiority or inferiority, beauty or ugliness or logic of a language variety, which are held to be irrelevant at the level of language system, acquire a very important and stratifying role at the level of use (Milroy and Milroy, 1991).

Standardisation

It is the most prestigious language variety that undergoes the process of codification involved in the production of a standard language variety (Montgomery, 1995). A standard variety becomes a supposedly unified and well-defined linguistic system. Prescriptive grammar books, guides to usage, dictionaries, and so on, through an elaborate process of codification, promote the standard system and create the correct form of usage (Montgomery, 1995). However, when this standard language variety is examined from a Foucaultian perspective, asymmetrical power relations carried in the production and outcome of this discourse are exposed. The distance from the standard relates in a significant way to the distance from the power base. The superior role of the standard variety, in practice, is socially ascribed. The standard is sanctioned by powerful institutions and groups within society and thus is accorded prestige. Its existence has resulted from an acceptance, mainly by powerful dominant groups, of a common core of linguistic conventions or norms (Milroy and Milroy, 1991). The standard variety becomes part of the ordered system of procedures for the production, regulation, distribution, circulation and operation of statements (Foucault, 1980). In this way it becomes an integral part of the general politics of truth.

Standard dialect is simply another dialect, no more, no less. It is neither linguistically superior to (Milroy and Milroy, 1991), nor aurally more refined than, other varieties (Edwards, 1989). The notions of excellence, purity and vulnerability of the standard variety are noted characteristics of all standard varieties (Hymes, 1974). There is a general feeling that the language will suffer if the standard is allowed to slip. It is believed that language is always on the downhill path and that it is up to experts such as lexicographers and grammarians to arrest and reverse this decline (Milroy and Milroy, 1991). The main value behind a wide variety of methods of language management is to function as a normative frame of reference to guide speakers (Downes 1984). The managers of the norms of language are part of the dominant class in societies and therefore are in a prime position to facilitate their own group.

Social class, language and education

One of the chief guardians (or 'language managers') of the norm is the education system (Edwards, 1989). As an institution the school functions to provide children with the standard language variety. Teachers aid in the development and proliferation of a homogeneous form of usage, known as the standard, which is the direct result of codification (Downes, 1984). This code sustains the norm. When there is a linguistic choice to be made (for example, between 'different from'/'different to'), 'language managers' usually recommend one as correct. This choice is often arbitrary in linguistic terms. The other variant would be quite serviceable. It does not have a superior logic, the choice is guided by the usage of certain group of people at the time (Milroy and Milroy, 1991). The code is merely based on the usage of the educated and socially prestigious members of the community (Holmes, 1992).

The ability to speak is almost universal and therefore not distinctive. The competence necessary in order to speak the legitimate language 'depends on social inheritance' (Bourdieu, 1991: 55). Schools and teachers are clearly implicated in rewarding this social inheritance and the relations of domination formed as a result of this inheritance. Bourdieu outlines the ability of a language variety to differentiate people socially. He links linguistic differences to social and economic differences pointing to a hierarchical universe of deviations with respect to a form of speech that is almost universally recognised as legitimate, that is, as the 'standard measure of linguistic products' (Bourdieu, 1991: 56).

Bourdieu and Passeron (1977) argue that schools trade in exclusive cultural capital. Those who possess the dominant form of cultural capital will have skills in the use of symbols, such as language and structures of meaning, defined as socially legitimate by the dominant culture. Since educational achievement is determined largely by the ability to perform in meritocratic tests that measure the skills provided by the dominant forms of cultural capital, students with access to such cultural capital, primarily through their families, will tend to do well in school.

It is clear, therefore, that education does not serve all equally and that a large number of the working class are marginalised as a result of the bias of the system. The degree of marginality experienced by the working class is described in Lynch and O'Riordan (1996). This compelling account of educational inequality in Ireland outlines the economic difficulties of the working class in attending higher education. It also details the bias in the education system. '(The) lifestyle, culture, values mores of the working class are not reflected in the curriculum' (Lynch and O'Riordan, 1996: 36).

The education system demands what it does not teach. This is mainly a linguistic and cultural competence which, arguably, can be produced only by one's background (Bourdieu, 1990). The working-class language system and culture are devalued and a deficit view of a working-class child's language and culture within the educational system often results in problems for the working-class child. The educational problems of the working class child can often be explained in terms of the institutional devaluation of such children's speech styles. In fact, some theorists would go so far as to say that all educational failure is linguistic failure (Stubbs, 1983).

The role of teachers

By virtue of their predominantly middle-class backgrounds (Kelly, 1970; O'Sullivan, 1980; Clancy, 1995), teachers are predisposed by their training and, indeed, by of all of their educational experience to promote values and attitudes consistent with these backgrounds. They are, after all, successful end-products of the system. In this way the education system continues to serve the classes or groups from whom it derives its authority (Bourdieu and Passeron, 1977). In Ireland this bias among teachers must be further examined in conjunction with the meritocratic, functionalist nature of the country's system of education which has for many years, it has been argued (Drudy and Lynch, 1993), fostered and assured the individualisation of educational failure. In this perspective the likelihood of fundamental change seems limited.

In relation to language and teachers' sensitivity to language varieties, Cheshire states that 'the most important factor here is a sympathetic awareness by the teacher of the nature of dialect difference' (Cheshire, 1991: 53). Negative teacher attitudes towards the speech of socially and culturally different children undoubtedly affect teacher expectations (Rist, 1970). Willis points out that 'one of the most oppressive forces is the belittling and sarcastic attitude of some teachers' (Willis, 1977: 77). The rejection of one's language variety is tantamount to a class insult and has grave consequences. In particular, it affects pupil performance (Edwards, 1989). There is a general, long-standing finding of research that teachers' perceptions of children's non-standard speech produces negative expectations about the children's personalities, social backgrounds and academic abilities (Giles, 1987, in Corson, 1994). Teachers have a very important role in the evaluation of children. Language often provides the chief basis of assessment with the result that lack of tolerance by teachers of non-standard language varieties may have grave implications for assessment (Milroy and Milroy, 1991). Although knowledge of this correspondence is widely acknowledged, it has not lessened the injustice in practice (Corson, 1994).

Children's response to language variation

Following theoretical analysis of the topic, I wish next to present some findings on the issue of language use in schools based on recent research. For the purposes of this chapter, I propose to concentrate on the responses to language variation of children themselves. The findings of the research indicate a clear difference between the experience of the middle-class child and the working-class child with the language expectations of the school. The attitudes, perceptions and hostilities of many of the working-class to the language environment of the school were remarkable. These findings are consistent with previous research on the implications for children where a language variety is viewed negatively by the school. While the comments reported here provide a clear picture of the children's feelings on the subject, they cannot represent the often scathing tone used by the children in working-class areas to express their anger.

CHILD	They want us t' be like them.
RESEARCHER	Why?
CHILD	Because they think they're better than us . . . they think they're higher up.
CHILD	No, yeh don't come t' school t' get yer language changed.
CHILD	It's your way o' speaking.
RESEARCHER	Do you think teachers should try and talk like you?
CHILD	It i'd be easier t' understan' them if they did.
CHILD	There's a whole class full tha' has t' talk like her an' jus' one tha' needs t' talk like us.
CHILD	No one stoppin' her from being posh.
RESEARCHER	How do you feel when they try t' change things?
CHILD	Yeh jus' pretend and then when yer ou' yeh say wha' yeh like.

Another clear issue that arises from these data is the high level of awareness that children have of language varieties. The importance of the language variety in the lives of children demands that more attention be paid to what children have to say about this aspect of school life.

CHILD We say 'Steveo', you say 'Steven' – you're different, even there.

The comments of the children reveal a strong negative feeling towards the language of the textbooks and a distinct lack of interest in such language variety. This attitude is not specific to children from any of the socio-economic groups. However, there is a difference in the nature of the 'anti-language attitude' that corresponds to the social class of the child. The working-class child has more of a problem in relation to understanding the language in the textbooks. This is a matter for concern for those involved in education and perhaps it is one of the causes of educational failure. This variety is very different and contains structure and vocabulary not included in the child's language repertoire. This puts the working-class child at a distinct disadvantage educationally. The degree of similarity between the language of the textbooks and the language ability of the middle-class child is further evidence that supports Bourdieu's and Passeron's (1977) theories of the suitability of middle-class linguistic capital in schools.

The children in the working-class schools had a very clear reason for not wanting to use the school language. This was not as evident or clearly articulated in the middle-class areas.

CHILD When yer in school yeh have t' try an' be posh an all tha' when yer out a school yeh can relax.

CHILD It's like two different lives.

CHILD They are here to teach us – not to tell us what to say.

CHILD We should talk the way we want to . . . it's our language.

CHILD Why should we not be able to talk the way we want to talk? . . . They're up in the staffroom talkin' the way they want to.

CHILD We want to talk the way our parents talk not the way the teachers talk.

The children were offered an alternative to the traditional textbook in the form of a schoolbook called *Get a Grip*. The discussion, which followed the reading of this text, revealed further attitudes about school and language variation. The children, irrespective of social class, reacted very favourably to the text. There were many reasons offered by the children as to why they preferred this vernacular.

CHILD	They're no' big mad words
CHILD	They're not the words that yer opposed t' speak
RESEARCHER	Who says they're not the words you're supposed to speak?
CHILD	Because, 'Ma' an' all that sort, really is real words
CHILD	They're slang words.
CHILD	It's better to say 'Mother'
RESEARCHER	If you went home to your house and said 'Mother' what would she say?
CHILD	She'd laugh.
CHILD	My Ma 'id say 'did you bang yourself or somethin?'
CHILD	I'd love it. I'd always want to do it.
CHILD	I'd get up in the mornin' to come in an' do tha'.
CHILD	I'd come to school every day.
CHILD	I'd do me homework.

Attitude to correction

As a result of the linguistic demands of the school, children have to adjust their language in order to comply with the demands of the school. This compliance is more difficult for the children of the working classes but is also experienced by the middle-class children. As a result, the level of correction in the schools is different. In general the working-class children were corrected more for the words they used and they way they spoke, while the children in the middle-class school were corrected for issues relating to good manners and for using slang. It is clear that policies of correction play a key role in forming negative attitudes towards school among the working class. Attempts at correction are viewed by the children as attempts to change their language. It is here that the prestige and the sense of solidarity with the language variety of the environment is most evident. The children seem to appreciate fully that, in correcting their language variety, the school system is not accepting or affirming their linguistic background.

CHILD	If yer tellin' her a story or somethin' an ye say somethin' wrong, she turns round and sez, she butts in on the story, it wrecks yer head.
RESEARCHER	Why does it wreck your head?
CHILD	Yeh want tell your story.
CHILD	Yer talkin your way an' she butts in an yeh forget where yeh are.
CHILD	They should jus' let yeh finish.
CHILD	She always tryin to correct us the way we talk like, when we say 'me Ma' she changes it.
CHILD	You pronounce yer 't's , you talk like her.
RESEARCHER	If you keep getting corrected, why don't you change the way you talk?
CHILD	'Cause we don't want t'.
CHILD	That's the way we talk.
CHILD	That's the way everybody talks around here. If you were to say compu-*ter* you'd probably get a baytin' or somethin'.
CHILD	When I put Ma down she puts a circle round it.
CHILD	If yeh write what you speak she scribbles it all out.
CHILD	Because say yeh say 'stall i', she'd give out t' yeh an' that's what yeh always say at home like.

Covert prestige

In accordance with the notion of covert prestige (Milroy, 1980; Montgomery, 1995), the children in the working-class areas have made a choice not to use the language of the school outside the school environment. This decision is based on a high level of awareness among the children of linguistic difference and a keen awareness of the consequences of changing language varieties. The main issue arising out of these findings is the sense of belonging to a group and the symbolic role language plays in defining this sense of solidarity with the group. It is interesting to note that attempts at being 'posh' are clearly discouraged by the children of the working classes. The feeling that to be posh would result in getting physically hurt is very strong among the working-class children.

CHILD   You'd sound tougher to yer posh cousins.

CHILD   They'd be afraid of yeh cause we're all common
             people.

CHILD   You'd sound like a nerd.

CHILD   You'd sound real posh.

Considering that the level of awareness of linguistic variation is very high among children, it is not surprising that attitudes to this variation are clearly defined. All children share a keen awareness of the implications of the different language varieties. They are aware of the link between occupational success, success in the education system and the prestige-bearing language code. They also view the middle-class language code as a basis for success in what they consider to be prestige-bearing employment. The research suggests that the prejudices of the society, carried through language variation and stratification, have been reproduced very effectively.

Conclusion

The comments and opinions of the working-class children reveal a high level of discontinuity between the home and the school with regard to language. The children fully appreciate the lack of value accorded to the working-class vernacular. The findings suggest that the children have constructed attitudes about their own vernacular that show evidence of low expectations regarding the types of employment available to them because of their language variety. Despite this there is a strong sense of solidarity towards, and covert prestige ascribed to, the working-class vernacular. It would seem that by continuing to ignore this language variety, the school is serving to sustain the discontinuous relations between itself and the working-class child. It is middle-class criteria of language and culture that provide the norm for making cultural judgements. The evidence from what has been reported in this chapter and from the whole research project indicates strongly that differential experience of the various socio-economic groups within the education system follows a similar pattern to that reported in international research. Despite many breakthroughs in the struggle for educational equality the fundamental issue of discontinuity remains unresolved. How can educationalists evaluate a culture they do not understand? How can they try to understand that culture, if the language necessary to express that culture is neither recognised nor encouraged ?

There are no 'big mad answers' or instant solutions to the issues raised in this paper. The debate surrounding the implications of language variation in education is far too complex to be so easily resolved. However, the issue is not served well by educationalists who react to the question of language variation by defending the tried and tested *status quo* and who remain entrenched in their defence of the standard language system. Nor can much be achieved by abandoning standards and language teaching altogether. Informed and pedagogically sound recommendations for the teaching of English, especially to those who are marginalised as a result of their culture and language variety, are needed. This should be a central part of any policy focused on combating educational inequality and should also provide a sound theoretical framework for future developments in this area.

References

Bourdieu, P. (1990) *In Other Words*, California: Stanford University Press.

Bourdieu, P. (1991) *Language and Symbolic Power*, edited by J.B. Thompson, Cambridge: Polity.

Bourdieu, P. and J. C. Passeron (1977) *Reproduction in Education, Society and Culture*, London: Sage.

Burr, V., (1995) *An Introduction to Social Constructionism*, London: Routledge.

Cheshire, J. (1991) 'Dialect features and linguistic conflict in schools.' *Language and Education*, 4 (4): 261–92.

Clancy, P. (1995) *Access to College: Patterns of Continuity and Change*, Dublin: Higher Education Authority.

Corson, D.J. (1990) *Language Policy Across the Curriculum*, Clevedon: Multilingual Matters.

Corson, D.J. (1994) 'Minority social groups and nonstandard discourse: towards a just language policy.' *The Canadian Modern Language Review*, 50 (2): 270–95.

Downes, W. (1984) *Language and Society*, London: Fontana.

Drudy, S. and K. Lynch, (1993) *Schools and Society in Ireland*, Dublin: Gill & Macmillan.

Edwards, A. (1989) *Language and Disadvantage*, 2nd edn, London: Edward Arnold.

166   Challenges of non-standard English

Edwards, J. (1985) *Language, Society and Identity*, New York: Blackwell.
Foucault, M. (1980) *Power/Knowledge, Selected Interviews and Other Writings*, ed. C. Gordon, London: Harvester Wheatsheaf.
Holmes, J. (1992) *An Introduction to Sociolinguistics*, London: Longman.
Hymes, D. (1974) *Foundations in Sociolinguistics*, London: Tavistock.
Kelly, S. (1970) *Teaching in The City*, Dublin: Gill & Macmillan.
Lynch, K. and C. O'Riordan (1996) *Social Class, Inequality and Higher Education: Barriers to Equality of Access and Participation among School Leavers*, Dublin: Equality Studies Centre, UCD.
Mac Ruairc, G. (1997) 'Big, mad words' – Perspectives of Language Variation in Schools: A Sociological Analysis'. Unpublished Med thesis, Education Department, UCD.
Milroy, L. (1980) *Language and Social Networks*, Oxford: Basil Blackwell.
Milroy, L. and J. Milroy (1991) *Authority in Language* (2nd edn), London/New York: Routledge.
Montgomery, M. (1995) *An Introduction to Language and Society*, 2nd edn, London: Routledge.
O' Sullivan, D. (1980) 'Teachers views on the effects of the home.' *Educational Research*, 22 (2): 138–42.
Richardson, P. (1991) 'Language as a personal resource and as a social construct: competing views of literacy pedagogy in Australia.' *Educational Review*, 43 (2).
Rist, R. (1970) 'Student social class and teacher expectations : the self fulfilling prophecy in ghetto education.' *Harvard Educational Review*, 40 (3): 411–51.
Saussure, F. de (1974) *Course in General Linguistics*, London: Fontana.
Stubbs, M. (1983) *Language, Schools and Classrooms*, 2nd edn, London: Methuen.
Trudgill, P. (1977) *Accent Dialect and the School*, London: Edward Arnold.
Wilkinson, A. and P. Trudgill (1977) in P. Trudgill *Accent Dialect and the School*, London: Edward Arnold.
Willis, P. (1977) *Learning to Labour*, Hampshire: Gower.

Appendix

The following is a brief account of the full research project referred to in this chapter. The larger research project focused on teachers and children in six different schools across the social class spectrum. The criteria used in the selection of teachers allowed for the examination of attitudes and practices in relation to language varieties between teachers working in the different schools with respect to this socio-economic difference. Teachers were interviewed and the design of the questions allowed for elaboration when the teacher or the researcher felt the issue raised by the question needed elaboration. The questions were designed to examine (*a*) teachers' attitude to, and awareness of, language varieties and (*b*) aspects of classroom policy and practice in relation to language variation.

The format used with the different groups of children was divided into two parts. The first part involved the administration of a standardised English test. The second section was divided into two subsections. Subsection one consisted of a discussion based on the language of the test and general questions about the language of textbooks and the language climate in the school. The second subsection involved the use of a text written in vernacular Dublin English. The text used was a selection from *Get a Grip*. This book is one of a series which were written by Paul Burton and was developed for use in Saint Laurence O Toole's Special School in Dublin. This text was used to promote further discussion on language varieties and to probe more deeply into the attitudes and perceptions of children in relation to the differences between language varieties. The main issues discussed referred to: School language versus home language; Awareness and use of style-shifting; Awareness of and reactions to differing language varieties; and, Attitude to correction and language environment of the school. For further detail, see Mac Ruairc, 1997.

Part 6

Adult literacy

15

Levels of literacy in Ireland:
the educational system
and the general population

Mark Morgan

The International Adult Literacy Survey (IALS) (Morgan, Hickey and Kellaghan, 1997) provides a profile of the literacy skills and practices of Irish adults, aged 16–65 years, compared with similar samples in eight other counties. The emerging picture poses challenges to the educational system and provides guidelines as to what might be the most fruitful policy directions in relation to literacy, over the next decade. Here the main findings of the IALS are summarised and an attempt is made to link some aspects of the findings with aspects of the educational system as these have come to light in research on features of the primary and second-level systems. Particular attention is given to the following issues: (i) How do older Irish adults compare with relatively younger age-groups in terms of literacy performance? (ii) What is the reason for the relatively poor performance of Irish people on higher-order cognitive skills? (iii) How does literacy influence features of life and leisure? (iv) How important is quantitative literacy in everyday life? (v) What is the association between early school leaving and literacy skills, and (vi) What is the reason for the low involvement of Irish people in adult education?

Measurement of literacy in the IALS

Rather than divide the population crudely into people who are 'literate' and those who are 'illiterate', the IALS sought to identify different levels – five in all – of literacy skill categories. [See Appendix, p. 178, for details of the IALS levels.] Furthermore, the following scales were used to cover the literacy demands at work, in the home and the community: (i) Prose literacy – the knowledge and skills required to understand and use information from newspapers, fiction and expository text; (ii) Document literacy – the knowledge and skills that are required to locate and use the information contained in official forms, timetables, maps, and charts, and (iii) Quantitative literacy – the knowledge and skills required to apply mathematical operations in printed materials. Within each domain of literacy the tasks ranged from simply locating information that was supplied to going beyond the information and making inferences in order to produce new information.

Each respondent was also given a background questionnaire which consisted of items on general information and background information on labour force participation, the kind of work carried out and on reading and writing at work. Other parts of the questionnaire were concerned with involvement with adult education or training, the kind of education involved and by whom the course was provided. Respondents were also asked about frequency of reading and writing in everyday life including visiting libraries and writing letters. They were also asked about the extent to which they needed help from time to time in filling forms and in reading instructions and similar activities.

What picture of literacy emerges from the IALS?

As noted above, the scores in the IALS are given in terms of levels of skills, rather than in simple categorisation of literate vs illiterate. People who score at Level 1 are able to perform at best only the simplest of tasks, typically those that require the readers to locate a single piece of information in the text, when there is no distracting information and when the structure of the text assists the search. Over the three domains of literacy, about 25 per cent of the Irish population were found to score at Level 1. This indicates that for one-quarter of the Irish adult population, this kind of simple literacy task is the limit of what they can do.

At the other end of the skill continuum Levels 4 and 5 (treated together in this report), require that the readers make inferences based on the information given, or integrate information from different parts of a lengthy text which usually contains plausible distracting information while the level of information given is much more abstract than in the case of lower levels. Roughly one-sixth of the Irish population scored at Levels 4/5 in the IALS.

Overall, it should be stressed that while it is not being said that one-quarter of the Irish population is 'illiterate', it is true that a very significant percentage have problems with all but the very simple literacy tasks. Equally it is of concern that only a small percentage of the population are at the highest levels of literacy, given that the tasks at these levels are of a kind that might be encountered in everyday life and work.

In comparing Ireland with the other countries in the study, it is important to realise that many of the participating countries are among the most socially and economically advanced. At the same time, the results are quite disappointing. For one thing, the percentage of Irish participants who are at the lowest level of literacy is highest of all the countries with the exception of Poland. At the same time it is worth stressing that in some countries (e.g. the US) around one-fifth of the population are also at Level 1 on the various scales. On the other hand only about ten per cent of people in the Netherlands were found to be at Level 1, while in Sweden just six per cent of adults were at this level.

It is of interest to note that since the Irish results were published in October 1977, the results of a national sample for the UK have also become available (OECD, 1997). In general, the results for the UK indicate that while the scores are marginally better than for Ireland, the difference falls within the margin of error associated with the estimates. Thus, while about 23 per cent of the UK population are at Level 1, this cannot be considered to be statistically significantly different from the corresponding estimate for Ireland. This same report, however, indicates that the scores for Australia, New Zealand, and Belgium are much better than those for the UK and for Ireland (OECD, 1997).

Age and level of education

It is not uncommon to hear people complain that standards in education have deteriorated. It is claimed that pupils leaving primary school a generation ago were better educated and more 'literate' than those leaving in recent times. While the IALS does not offer definitive evidence on this point, it is an interesting outcome that age is very strongly and negatively associated with literacy performance. In general the greatest differences are between the younger age groups and those aged 46 years and over. For example, 17 per cent of people aged between 16 and 25 years are at Level 1 (documents scales), while for those aged 26–35 years the percentage is rather similar (20 per cent). However, the percentage of adults who score at this level is much greater in the age-group 46–55 years (36.1 per cent), while in the oldest age group in the survey (55–65 years) the percentage scoring at Level 1 is 44.1 per cent. Furthermore, there are corresponding differences at the highest level of literacy performance.

There are two explanations for these differences. One is in terms of aging *per se* that is, that a decline in cognitive performance takes place as people get older. Another explanation is that older cohorts are less well educated, thus accounting for the dramatic differences. It is interesting that longitudinal studies that have followed particular groups from young adulthood to old age, have found little evidence that aging *per se* has a strong influence on cognitive performance until age 65 and older (Schaie, 1994). However, there are very dramatic differences in the age of leaving school and the educational qualifications of those aged 45 and over compared with the younger age-groups. It is very likely that these educational differences are a major influence on the pattern observed in the IALS.

Performance on higher-order skills

Because the conceptualisation of literacy in the IALS ranged from elementary decoding tasks to complex cognitive activities involving inference and interpretation, it was possible to see how Irish adults rate on such higher order skills. It is especially disappointing that only 13.5 per cent scored at Levels 4/5 in prose literacy, 11.5 per cent in document literacy and 16 per cent in quantitative literacy.

This pattern of poor performance in higher order skills is found in international studies of the school population in various areas of the curriculum. For example, in the study of mathematics in 14 systems, it was found that while Irish children did well in basic numeracy skills, they did relatively less well in higher order tasks like problem solving (Martin, Hickey and Murchan, 1993). Furthermore, in the IEA Literacy study it was found that Irish teachers placed relatively greater emphasis on basic skills like word recognition and simple comprehension than they did on broader aims like expanding world views and critical thinking (Martin and Morgan, 1994).

Literacy skills, work and leisure

It is well known that young people leaving school without qualifications are likely to encounter difficulties in the labour market. On these grounds, it might be expected that literacy competence effects would extend to employment and earnings and this turned out to be the case. What was more remarkable, however, was the way in which literacy skills were found to exert an influence in domains of people's lives that might not be assumed to be associated with literacy practices. It is of particular interest to find that involvement in literacy activities is associated with several non-literacy activities including participation in sport, attendance at plays, films, concerts as well as participating in community organisations. Thus, it would seem that literacy activity and competence are associated with a richer and fuller involvement in a range of activities. On the other hand, sustained television viewing is negatively associated with both literacy and non-literacy activities.

In this regard, it is a particular concern that while some literacy practices (e.g. newspaper reading) are engaged in by almost all of the population, a significant minority of adults are never involved in any notable literacy activity. Specifically one-fifth of people never read a book and an even greater number never write anything substantial. This is likely to be related to competence since one of the ways in which competence is enhanced is through challenging activities. Another consequence of this non-involvement in literacy activities is for inter-generational effects; there is ample evidence that literacy competence is greatly enhanced where young children are exposed to a 'literacy environment' from a young age (Elley, 1992).

Quantitative literacy

As noted above the IALS included tests not only of prose and document literacy but also of quantitative literacy, specifically on the knowledge and skills required to apply arithmetic information. A number of factors influence the difficulty of tasks in the quantitative literacy domain including difficulty of the printed information, the number of arithmetic operations involved, the extent to which numbers are embedded in printed materials and the degree to which inferences must be made in order to identify the particular kind of arithmetic operation involved.

A particularly interesting finding from the IALS was that people in all occupations are involved in mathematical activities more frequently than in literacy activities. Even in relatively unskilled occupations, the percentage who say that they are frequently involved in activities like estimating or measuring size/weight or calculating prices is greater than for any single kind of literacy activity. It is also of interest that when asked to assess their skills in relation to others, rather more people said that their mathematical skills were moderate or poor than for other skills. Just 19 per cent of the workers said that their mathematical skills were 'moderate' or 'poor', while the corresponding for reading and writing were 8.6 per cent and 11.7 per cent, respectively.

In general, people's assessment of their skills tended to err on the optimistic side. When asked whether their skills were limiting their advancement at work, only a small percentage (over five per cent) took the view that this was the case. However, many people who thought that their skills were adequate and were not limiting their chances of advancement had very poor literacy skills, as indicated by their performance on the actual tests. This suggests a lack of awareness of the need to improve their skills and may partly explain the low involvement in adult education especially by people with limited literacy skills.

Early school leaving, literacy performance and related experiences

Because the IALS obtained information from respondents on age of school leaving, it was possible to provide a profile of the experiences of adults who had left school having completed the junior secondary cycle only (and indeed without having completed this cycle). As might be expected the literacy performance of these adults was poor indeed. More than three-fifths of people who had left school without completing the junior cycle were at Level 1, while less than two per cent were at the highest levels. As found in earlier studies, these early school leavers were much more likely to be unemployed.

It is especially interesting that relatively more early school leavers had lower self-ratings of their literacy skills and they were also more likely to say that deficiencies in their skills were limiting their opportunities for advancement at work. It is also significant that early school leaving was associated with a restricted range of activities both with regard to literacy and non-literacy activities.

Given that the IALS did not have any longitudinal information, the role of literacy problems in the series of events leading to early school leaving must be a matter of conjecture. However, there is evidence that a significant minority of children can be identified in primary school, who are unlikely to be able to cope with the literacy demands of the second level system. In the early study of Fontes and Kellaghan (1977) this minority was calculated to be about 6–8 per cent. Interestingly, more recent calculations place the figure at roughly the same percentage (Morgan and Martin, 1994). One possibility is that the failure in all subjects resulting from literacy problems causes a degree of alienation and sense of failure that leads eventually to quitting school at the first opportunity.

Adult education

Participation in adult education/training was much lower in Ireland than in the other countries in the study. Most participants in adult education paid for their own courses and this was even more likely in the case of women. The single most frequent goal of courses taken was the up-grading of careers, but a high percentage had also taken courses leading to formal qualifications that are normally taken at second or third level. In line with this, many of the courses were located in schools and colleges that traditionally cater for second- and third-level students. Furthermore most of the methods of instruction involved conventional classroom techniques like lectures and workshops with relatively low levels of use of technological developments or 'on the job' training.

As found in earlier studies, level of education was particularly strongly associated with participation in adult education. Adults who had completed the Leaving Certificate course were about four times more likely to be involved in adult education than people who left school without having completed the Junior cycle, while college graduates were about six times as likely. In turn there was a strong association between literacy skills and participation in adult education with people at lower levels being unlikely to have taken any education/training. In fact, only about one-tenth of people at Level 1 had participated in education/training during the previous year.

While the low provision for adult education is one of the main reasons for the relatively low involvement of adults in education, some features of the primary and second-level systems are also relevant to the demand for such education. It is worth inquiring about the extent to which the system prepares students for life-long learning. In this regard, it is interesting that the IEA literacy study showed that access to library books was substantially lower in Irish schools than was the case in many other countries with a similar level of socio-economic development (Martin and Morgan, 1994). Coupled with this, independent reading was also lower, despite the fact that Irish students tend to spend relatively longer time in assigned work than students in other countries. Thus, it may be that the self-motivated learning may not be encouraged within the system, resulting in relatively lower demand for lifetime learning and adult education. The combination of low provision and demand may account for the pattern evident in the IALS.

Conclusions

There is need for a comprehensive approach to ensure that the literacy skills of Irish adults are in line with the demands of modern society. This will involve attention to reading problems in school as well as efforts to tackle adult literacy problems. However, it should be stressed that a 'back to basics' approach may be inappropriate since the main difficulties have to do with the large number of adults who can decode print but have difficulty with handling material of moderate complexity.

The findings of this and related studies indicate the importance of promoting the concept of lifelong learning. There is substantial evidence that adults' capacity to learn does not inevitably decline with age and that the age-related decline in test performance may be largely due either to lower levels of education or to the lack of opportunity to practise relevant skills. It is especially important that new structures give attention to those groups who are least likely to participate in adult education, especially people from disadvantaged backgrounds whose literacy skills are moderate to poor.

It is important that the current efforts to assist adults with literacy problems be broadened and strengthened. The present data indicate that the potential number of students for adult literacy programmes is very great indeed. In developing such programmes, there is a need to ensure that the learners' interests, background and motivation be taken into account so that adults who have experienced literacy difficulties should be enabled to take control of their learning. Given the IALS results it is especially important that there should not be a focus on a small group of 'illiterates'; rather the aim should be to assist the large number of people who have very moderate literacy skills and who seldom have any involvement in any substantial reading or writing activity.

References

Elley, W. (1992) *How in the World do Students Read?* The Hague: International Association for the Evaluation of Educational Achievement.

Fontes, P. and T. Kellaghan (1997) 'Incidence and correlates of illiteracy in Irish primary schools.' *Irish Journal of Education*, Vol. 11: 5–20.

Martin, M., Hickey, B.L. and D. Murchan (1992) 'The second international assessment of educational progress: mathematics and science findings in Ireland.' *Irish Journal of Education*, Vol. 26: 3–146.

Martin, M. and Morgan, M. (1994) 'Reading literacy in Ireland: a comparative analysis.' *Irish Journal of Education*, 28: 3–101.

Morgan, M., Hickey, B.L. and T. Kellaghan (1997) *International Adult Literacy Survey: Results for Ireland*. Dublin: Stationery Office.

Morgan, M. and M. Martin (1995) 'Reflections on the IEA literacy study.' In: Shiel, G., Ni Dhalaigh, U. and B.O'Reilly (eds), *Reading Development to Age 15: Overcoming Difficulties*, Dublin: Reading Association of Ireland.

Organisation for Economic and Social Development/Human Resources Development Canada (1997) *Literacy Skills for the Knowledge Society: Further Results from the International Adult Literacy Survey*. Paris: OECD.

Schaie, K.W. (1994). 'The course of adult intellectual development.' *American Psychologist*, 49: 304–13.

Appendix

IALS Levels: A Brief Outline

Level 1

The tasks at this level require the reader to locate a single piece of information in the text. Usually the information in the text is identical to or synonymous with the information asked for in the question or direction. In addition, the text has an organisational structure that assists the reader in the search for the information. If a possible incorrect answer is in the text, it tends not to be near the correct information. For example, one of the tasks at Level 1 asks respondents to look at the directions on a bottle of aspirin to find out 'the maximum number of days a person should take this medicine'. In the text, there is only a single reference to 'number of days' and the information is set out in headings.

Level 2

The tasks at Level 2 also ask respondents to locate information in the text. However, there are some factors that make these tasks more complex than Level 1. Relatively more information is sought, or the distracting information is more plausible, or several pieces of information must be integrated. For example, in one of the tasks readers are given information about the Impatiens plant, its origin, appearance, general care, watering, and diseases. One of the associated questions asks what happens when the plant is exposed to temperatures of 14 degrees centigrade or lower. The relevant answer is provided under the heading 'General care' in the second List sentence, which indicates that '. . . When the plant is exposed to temperatures of 12–14 degrees Centigrade, it loses its leaves and won't bloom any more.'

Level 3

The tasks at Level 3 are more difficult than those at Level 2 with respect to at least one of the following features. For some tasks, the reader is required to find several pieces of information that are located in different parts of the text. Other tasks require the reader to make comparisons or to integrate information from different parts of the text, and still others require readers to make relatively low-level inferences.

One task requiring low-level inference involves an article about cotton nappies. The reader is asked to list three reasons why the authors prefer cotton nappies to disposable ones. This task is relatively more difficult than those at earlier levels because of the need to provide several answers from different parts of the text and also because of the need to make inferences about the reasons, which are not simply listed. At no point in the text is the relevant information supplied literally; the reader has to work out the solutions that satisfy the requirements of the task.

Level 4

The tasks at Level 4 are more complex than those at the lower levels in a number of respects. Frequently they require readers to make text-based inferences. In other instances, the task involves integrating information from different parts of a lengthy text. In addition, the text usually contains plausible distracting information and the level of the information is more abstract.

In one task, readers were given information about various kinds of interview techniques and asked to describe in their own words 'one difference between the panel interview and the group interview.' The relevant information is not presented directly but can be inferred from the brief description of each kind of interview. Thus, to perform this task, the reader needs to understand the nature of each kind of interview and, based on this understanding, to note at least one point of difference.

Level 5

The tasks at this level are the most complex. Some require the reader to make high-level inferences from relatively difficult text and use specialised knowledge which they bring to the task. Other questions demand the ability to locate information in dense text which contains many plausible distractors.

In one task at Level 5, respondents are presented with an announcement from a company's personnel department about an initiative which was intended to help employees to search for another job inside, or outside, the company. The readers are asked to 'list two ways in which the initiative helps people who will lose their jobs because of a departmental reorganisation'. If readers were to answer correctly, they had to search through the text and locate the embedded sentence 'CIEM acts as a mediator for employees who are threatened with dismissal resulting from a reorganisation, and assists with finding new positions when necessary.' What makes this task difficult is that the style of the information being sought is different to that used in the text and the information is under the heading of 'mediation', which in turn is one of several headings, any of which might be plausible distractors.

16
Teaching literacy to adults

Annette Brady, Ursula Coleman
and Rosamond Phillips

Until the publication of *Education 2000* (Morgan, Hickey, and Kellaghan, 1997) the National Adult Literacy Agency (NALA) relied on estimates which suggested that between five per cent and 16 per cent of the adult population experienced some degree of literacy difficulty. The method used to compute these estimates was based on the traditional approach to defining being 'literate' in the Irish context as the completion of sixth class in primary school (DuVivier, 1991). Recent researchers, however, as the preceding chapter explains, have favoured a different approach to quantifying the problem in western industrialised countries. Rather than dividing a given population crudely into 'the literate' and 'the illiterate', the OECD International Adult Literacy Survey (IALS) sought to identify five levels of literacy to cover demands at home, at work, and in the community.

The Irish results of the survey show that approximately 25 per cent of the adult population (i.e. those between the ages of 16 and 64) were not able to get beyond Level 1 when tested (Morgan et al., 1997). The authors note: 'People who score at this level are able to perform at best, only the simplest of tasks, typically those that require the reader to locate a single piece of information in a text, when there is no distracting information and when the structure of the text assists the search' (p. vii). This percentage amounts to approximately 500,000 people. A further thirty per cent of the population could not get beyond Level 2, which required survey participants to locate, comprehend and integrate two or more pieces of information in a text which one might reasonably expect to encounter in everyday life.

Tasks at Level 3, which is considered the minimum desirable threshold in most industrialised countries, required the reader to integrate or compare several pieces of information from different parts of a relatively complex piece of text, and in some cases to make low-level inferences – i.e. to work out the appropriate answer from a text which does not supply the relevant information in a literal fashion. Approximately 16 per cent of the adult population scored at Levels 4 and 5, which were treated as a composite level in the report. Reading materials at these levels tended to be significantly more abstract than those used at the lower levels and sometimes included highly technical language. Readers were required to make inferences based on information in a text that usually contained plausible distracting information.

The aim of adult literacy provision

The need for literacy skills must be seen in the context of the culture and society in which we live. Rapidly changing economies require ever higher levels of literacy if people are to adapt and participate fully in society. Research has highlighted the role of parents, and particularly mothers, in structuring the educational environment within the home (Kellaghan et al., 1995). Adult students, themselves, tell us that their self-esteem and quality of life are negatively affected by poor literacy skills (Bailey and Coleman, 1998). Teaching literacy to adults is a specific field of practice with its own distinctive philosophy and methods. Our aim in the context of this paper is to share some ideas and insights with regard to the tutoring methods, the materials, and the type of environment which adults prefer when they are working on literacy skills.

Literacy is about more than reading and writing. Definitions range from those which place a narrow focus on skill development to those which emphasise the radical nature of literacy as a set of enabling skills which help adults to exercise greater choice and control in their lives. NALA suggests a definition of good adult literacy work which emerges from a respect for the whole person:

> All good adult literacy work starts with the needs of individuals. Literacy involves the integration of listening, speaking, reading, writing and numeracy. It also encompasses aspects of personal development – social, economic, emotional – and is concerned with improving self-esteem and building confidence. It goes far beyond mere technical skills of communication. The underlying aim of good literacy practice is to enable people to understand and reflect critically on their life circumstances with a view to exploring new possibilities and initiating constructive change. (NALA, 1995)

Literacy, in this sense, enables people to be independent in their daily lives, to make choices, to exercise to the full their role as parents, workers and citizens, and to be in a position to undertake further education and/or training with confidence.

Barriers to learning

Literacy providers have to take account of the range of barriers faced by adults with reading and writing difficulties. Experience over the years and recent research which involved interviews with literacy students throughout the country (Bailey and Coleman, 1998) show that adults who wish to return to basic education tend to encounter a range of barriers, among which are the following:

- Shame and embarrassment about their low level of educational attainment
- Low self-esteem and a lack of confidence in their ability to learn
- Fear of failure as a result of negative school experiences
- Fear of the formal system, e.g. schools, teachers, classes, tests
- Difficulty in accessing information about provision

Adult literacy provision, therefore, if it is to be successful, must address these barriers by establishing appropriate learning environments, and using suitable methodologies and materials.

It must also respect the adult status of the students and enable them 'to contribute their skills, knowledge and experience to the learning process' (NALA, 1991). The setting and atmosphere in which literacy tuition is offered can play an important part in encouraging adults to return to second chance education. Every effort is made to ensure that publicity material is sensitive and non-threatening and that the initial contact is informal and in the strictest confidence. Students who attend a literacy scheme, of which more than a hundred exist throughout Ireland, usually have the option of either one-to-one or small group tuition. They receive individual attention and share the responsibility of planning a learning programme with their tutor. In a group situation the emphasis is on collaborative learning rather than on a competitive atmosphere. Students appreciate this approach and gradually regain confidence in themselves as learners.

Materials

One of the most successful methods for developing reading and writing skills with beginners is the 'language experience' approach, a way of teaching reading that is based on the student's own spoken language, vocabulary and speech patterns. The student dictates a sentence or two to the tutor, who writes it down exactly as the student has said it. It then becomes a piece of reading material, containing adult ideas and vocabulary, which can be worked on in a variety of ways. This method guarantees both understanding and interest, key factors in helping a person to read. It enables students gradually to increase the number of words they can recognise by sight and also gives them the chance to work on their own writing from the start of tuition. Among its other advantages are: building confidence from the beginning by putting a value on the student's life experience; valuing the culture and language of each individual; and providing an imme-diate experience of success in that the student is more easily able to read his or her own material.

The language experience method can be used to develop reading and spelling skills with students at a variety of levels, depending on the length and complexity of the text generated. However, the use of other materials is also an important aspect of adult literacy work. Here again the focus must be on the needs and interests of the student. 'What would you like to be able to read?' or 'What do you need to write at the moment?' are the important questions for the tutor to ask. The student's answers help the tutor to decide what might be suitable material – e.g. various sections of a newspaper, a particular magazine, a holiday brochure, a driving licence application form, and so on. The tutor must also be able match the relative difficulty of a piece of text with the student's actual reading ability. If a student is keen to read a complex article on a particular topic, the tutor may decide to reproduce the article in a simplified version. This process of simplification involves keeping the meaning and key points of the article, but eliminating difficult vocabulary and the more complex forms of sentence construction.

Thus the materials used in the earlier stages of adult literacy work reflect the needs and interests of the individual student. There is no set textbook. The challenge for the tutor is to seek out, create or adapt existing materials which will be relevant and interesting to each individual.

Developing literacy skills to higher levels

Adult students who return to education have a variety of needs. Some are at a basic level and need individual or small group (from two to six) attention. Others present with different aims – to develop their reading skills, to write creatively, or to pursue a more formal programme such as Junior Certificate or Leaving Certificate English. Much of the work done by tutors, working with groups of adults in continuing education programmes, is in fact assisting students in their efforts to move up through the levels of literacy as defined in *Education 2000*. Literacy training in this context has a wide brief. It involves developing a range of skills and abilities: reading, vocabulary, writing, comprehension, a sensitivity to language and to the different registers of language, an understanding of sentence construction and punctuation, a basic grammatical competence, the ability to think through, infer, and bring a critical eye to the analysis of text. The development of such skills does not always occur explicitly in the context of language work; a great deal of it may in fact be addressed through explanation, discussion, and small group exercises while teaching literature.

In this type of work the method, approach, and skills of the tutor are crucially important. Once again it is the needs and interests of the students which must be addressed. Although a tutor may now be working with a much larger group (anything from eight to 20), it is still important that it be viewed as a learning group rather than as a class in the formal sense. Plenty of discussion time is necessary in the early stages. In this way students are encouraged to participate orally, to build up their trust in each other and in the tutor, and to share their experiences – whether about memories of their school days or preferences in reading material. Meanwhile the tutor is getting a sense of the group, finding out what people know and where the gaps in their knowledge and skills may be, and identifying the more vulnerable students – those who may drop out if their needs are not specifically addressed.

Second-chance students are often afraid of being left behind and this can happen all too easily if the emphasis is solely on content, on the covering of the course. For many adult students, testing, in the traditional sense, is not an appropriate method of assessment especially in the early stages of a course. For more vulnerable students it can often feel like being framed for failure. It can also create an atmosphere of competition within the group which is reminiscent of formal schooling. Some system of assessing progress is, of course, important as the course proceeds. When the curricular content begins to assume a more central role tutors must be vigilant to ensure that it does not take precedence over the learning process. They must constantly check with their students that the process is continuing to work for them. There is, in our view, no merit in covering the course if you have not been able to bring your group with you.

This approach to the teaching of English requires skill, sensitivity, flexibility and confidence on the part of the tutor. Above all, perhaps, it requires a belief that adults, for whom schooling was not an encouraging experience, can best recover confidence and begin to realise their potential, as learners, in a supportive, non-competitive atmosphere. Adult students appreciate this mode of teaching as the following account, written by Annette two years after sitting the Leaving Certificate English examination, illustrates:

I am the second eldest of fourteen children. Due to ill health my mother was unable to care for the younger children, so I was removed from school at fourteen years of age to help her. My memory wisely protects me from that period in my life, yet I have until recently maintained that I cried back then. Now I sense that they were silent tears, creating an ache within me for something that was lost, yet was entirely unvoiced and unfelt.

My memory of my school days is hazy. I liked book-keeping but wasn't able to draw. English is entirely forgotten. Between the ages of fourteen and nineteen I made two attempts to go nursing but my parents refused. Then my mother died and for another two years I continued to care for everybody in my family. At the age of twenty-one I finally went to England to start nursing. I remember my father helping me with some Maths before I went. It was only as I interacted with my classmates that I became somewhat conscious of my lack of education. After one examination, I remember the tutor shouting in such a superior voice that she had never seen such an attempt at spelling the word 'oesophagus' in her entire life. If the ground had opened that day I would gladly have dropped into the hole. Strangely I did pass the examination. Yet after about eight months I simply gave up. I then married and started having my family. After my first baby I decided to study Maths and English by correspondence. I paid my money and opened the books. I promptly closed them again – for almost twenty years. They were beyond me.

Yet unconsciously something was happening. As I encouraged my children through school I realised that I needed to do something for myself. I decided to do 'baby Maths' as I was not afraid of them. The Maths class was pure joy, made so by my classmates, but mostly by the teacher. Her ability was such that she catered to everybody's needs, yet encouraged us to move on when ready and able. Over three years I sat Junior and Leaving Certificate Maths. Then I enrolled in the Maynooth counselling course, but I ran into difficulties with English. I could express myself when speaking, but found it almost impossible to put pen to paper. Nonetheless I completed the first year. Then I enrolled for a one-year English course. I had heard about the 'brilliant English teacher'. How well I remember the poetry book! I couldn't even understand the questions, never mind answer them. I was unable to write even one full sentence. After two weeks I ran. I simply ran away. Essays and prose were flying over my head like they had wings.

Luckily for me I ran in the right direction. I ran to KLEAR, a community-based Adult Education Centre, where they provided a two-year course in English. I remember begging for a chance to join the class, which was already full. I had this sense that if I could achieve an A1 in Maths that I could still learn English. Thankfully my plea was heard. I got a place in the class. The next two years will stay forever in my memory – mostly because essays, exams or prose were never mentioned until I was well and truly hooked on learning for the sheer enjoyment of learning. Poetry! I was always able to recite poetry but never knew anything else about it other than that I liked the sound. Now I feel as if Patrick Kavanagh is my brother and Emily Dickinson my sister. Such a wonderful, astute teacher we had. Our first essay! If I remember correctly, she never said that dreaded word 'essay'. 'Go home and write a few lines about something you feel passionately about', she told us. I remember the essay well, Children's Rights. There were no time restrictions. One and a half pages of my soul poured onto paper. She had cleverly tapped into my deepest feelings. I had grown up in a family where children were meant to be seen and not heard. But I could speak and now I found that I could write. Perhaps some of the grammar was incorrect. But that was not my crime. It belongs with society!

My thirst for knowledge has increased rather than decreased with the years. I am unable to express in words the ache within my soul for something that in one sense is intangible, yet has dominated my life. If asked to describe what second-chance education meant to me I would feel compelled to reply – 'Food for my soul'. The teaching of English, for me, depended on the teacher fully realising that I lived in a world of silence – no expression of feelings – as did many of my generation. One really needs to tap into that reality before anything can be achieved. Perhaps you have read Seamus Deane's book, *Reading in the Dark*. To me it was music on paper. Without my teacher I would not have experienced that same sense of wonder. The only way forward in the teaching of English has to be the way it was taught to me, which was communication through discussion, laughter, and theatre. Our teacher had the 'plans' in her head and we learned to trust her. The similarity between my Maths teacher and my English teacher was that they both had the ability to reach each individual person irrespective of their different abilities.

Conclusion

Teaching literacy to adults, as we understand it, is essentially about developing the whole person. As human beings we do not simply learn language, we learn through language. 'Language', we are told by Brian Cox (see p. 25 above), quoting Sven Birkerts, 'is the soul's ozone layer and we thin it at our peril.' Many, many adults in today's Ireland have simply not had a chance to learn through language. And, as Annette's account poignantly illustrates, 'the soul's ozone layer' was indeed thinned for her and for many of her generation.

The teaching of literacy to adults already exists, in an Irish context, as a distinct field of practice. Its philosophy, its methods, its materials, its approach to preparation for examinations have been developed collaboratively from the ground up, with the involvement of adult students at every stage. This field of practice involves trained volunteers and professional educators working side by side within an organised and effective model of adult education, outside the established formal system. In our experience such an approach actually works for many adults for whom the more formal approach is, for a variety of reasons, inappropriate.

References

Bailey, I. and U. Coleman (1998) *Access and Participation in Adult Literacy Schemes*, Dublin: National Adult Literacy Agency.

DuVivier, E. (1991) 'How many illiterates? Towards an estimate of the incidence of reading and writing difficulties among Irish adults.' *Studies in Education*, Vol. 7: 7–28.

Kellaghan, T. Weir, S., O hUallachain, S. and M. Morgan (1995). *Educational Disadvantage in Ireland*, Dublin: Educational Research Centre /Combat Poverty Agency/Department of Education.

Morgan, M., Hickey, B. and T. Kellaghan (1997) *Education 2000*, Dublin: Educational Research Centre/Department of Education.

NALA (1991) *Guidelines for Good Adult Literacy Work*, Dublin: National Adult Literacy Agency.

OECD (1995) *Literacy, Economy and Society*, Paris: Organisation for Economic Cooperation and Development.

Notes on contributors

Annette Brady is a mature student who has recently completed the Trinity Access Programme. Ursula Coleman is a tutor, trainer and researcher in the field of Adult Basic and Continuing Education. Rosamond Phillips, formerly Assistant Director of the National Adult Literacy Agency (NALA), is now a freelance literacy trainer and practitioner.

Pat Coffey is a Senior Inspector with the Department of Education and Science. He is Chief Examiner for Leaving Certificate Higher Level English and for English and Communication in the Leaving Certificate Applied programme.

Valerie Coghlan is a College of Education librarian with extensive experience in the area of children's literature. She is a founding member of the Children's Literature Association of Ireland and a Trustee of the Irish Children's Book Trust.

Brian Cox was John Edward Taylor Professor of English at the University of Manchester until his retirement. He is now Chair of the North West England Arts Board and a member of the UK Arts Council. He was a founder-editor in 1959 of *Critical Quarterly*, and has published many critical books and articles. In 1989 he chaired the British National Curriculum English Working Group.

Brendan Culligan is a teacher who has specialised in Remedial Education for 15 years. He is a designer and tutor of inservice courses on Learning Difficulties – Literacy; and has lectured widely on literacy difficulties. He is the author of various articles on reading and spelling, most recently on improving children's spelling.

John Devitt has been Head of the English Department in Mater Dei Institute since 1979. He has written extensively on literary and educational topics and also has an interest in film and film history.

Mary Howard taught drama for several years before retraining as a primary teacher. She wrote a thesis on the work of Augusto Boal as part of a postgraduate degree in Modern Drama Studies and she now works as a primary teacher.

James Kavanagh is a primary schools inspector in the Department of Education and Science. He has recently been awarded a PhD from University College Dublin for his research on the teaching of compositional writing in the primary school.

Declan Kiberd, Professor of Anglo-Irish Literature and Drama at University College Dublin, has lectured on Irish culture, language and literature in more than twenty countries. His many publications include *Inventing Ireland* (Jonathan Cape, 1995).

Gerry Mac Ruairc is a primary teacher who has worked in Tallaght for the past 15 years. His chapter is based on research relating to an MEd dissertation submitted in University College Dublin, July 1997.

Robert Mohr lectures on writing in various departments at University College Dublin, to adult students in Adult Education also at UCD, to professionals, and to deaf adults, NUI, Maynooth.

Mark Morgan is a lecturer in psychology and researcher at St Patrick's College, Dublin. His chapter draws on the International Adult Literacy Survey which was funded by the Department of Education and was carried out at the Educational Research Centre at St Patrick's College, Dublin.

Tom Mullins is a senior lecturer in Education at University College Cork. He is education officer for the NCCA English syllabus committees and has been instrumental in the development of the revised English syllabi at both Junior and Leaving Certificates.

Elizabeth O'Gorman is a secondary teacher with involvement in learning support and an interest in teacher education. She has previously worked with the Curriculum Development Unit and lectured in the Institute of Education, Hong Kong.

Ann Whelan is an educational psychologist working in private practice. She also lectures part-time in special needs education at University College Dublin. She has read a number of papers on her field of study to conferences in Ireland and abroad.

Kevin Williams lectures in the Mater Dei Institute of Education, and is a past President of the Educational Studies Association of Ireland. He is author/editor of several books and has published many articles on philosophical and educational issues.

Index